THE MYTH OF ABILITY

ALSO BY JOHN MIGHTON

Scientific Americans

Possible Worlds

A Short History of Night

Body and Soul

The Little Years

The Myth of Ability

Nurturing Mathematical Talent in Every Child

John Mighton

ANANSI

Published in 2003 by
House of Anansi Press Inc.
110 Spadina Avenue, Suite 801
Toronto, ON, M5V 2K4
Tel. 416-363-4343
Fax 416-363-1017
www.anansi.ca

Distributed in Canada by
Publishers Group Canada
250A Carlton Street
Toronto, ON, M5A 2L1
Tel. 416-934-9900
Toll free order numbers:
Tel. 800-663-5714   Fax 800-565-3770

07   06   05   04   03   1   2   3   4   5

National Library of Canada Cataloguing in Publication Data

Mighton, John, 1957–
The myth of ability : nurturing mathematical
talent in every child / John Mighton.

ISBN 0-88784-693-9

1. Junior Undiscovered Mathematical Prodigies.
2. Mathematics—Study and teaching (Elementary) 3. Mathematical ability.
4. Children with social disabilities—Education. 5.Underachievers.
6. Mighton, John, 1957– I. Title.

QA135.6 M535 2003   372.7   C2003-901606-4

Cover design: Bill Douglas @ The Bang
Page design & composition: PageWave Graphics Inc.

The Canada Council | Le Conseil des Arts
for the Arts | du Canada
since 1957 | depuis 1957

*We acknowledge for their financial support of our publishing program the Canada Council for the Arts,
the Ontario Arts Council, the Government of Ontario through the Ontario Media Development
Corporation's Ontario Book Initiative, and the Government of Canada through the
Book Publishing Industry Development Program (BPIDP).*

Printed and bound in Canada

To the students and volunteers of JUMP,
whose efforts made this book possible

Contents

Introduction

IMAGINE A SCHOOL WHERE THE FOLLOWING RITUAL IS OBSERVED. At the end of the year, after several days of coaching and preparation, the children are led to a cafeteria where tables have been set with plates of food, one for each child. A government official has inspected the plates; for a given grade each plate holds exactly the same foods, in the same proportions, at the same temperatures. To encourage a feeling of fair play and sportsmanship, the children have been instructed not to touch their knives or forks until everyone is comfortably seated. At a signal from a teacher, the children begin eating, madly trying to stuff as much food into their mouths as they can before a buzzer signals that the meal is over. Afterwards, the children are given a battery of tests to determine how well they are digesting their food.

Now imagine that only those children judged to be superior eaters are allowed to eat a full and balanced diet at school the following year. The teachers at the school, though well-meaning, believe only a few children are born with the capacity to digest food properly; the rest, depending on what kind of stomach they've inherited, can eat only one or two kinds of food, and even then only in small quantities. When challenged to defend this belief, the teachers point to the vast number of weak and unhealthy students at the school: even those singled out for special attention continue to complain of stomach disorders when placed on restricted diets.

One day people will look back on our present system of education as only slightly more rational or humane than this. A great deal of recent research in early childhood education has begun to show that, with very few exceptions, children are born capable of learning anything. Unfortunately, the existence of this research has done little to change the way children are being taught, at home or at school.

In 1998, when I was in the final year of a doctoral program in mathematics (a subject I had struggled with as a child), I persuaded several of my friends to start an educational charity called JUMP (Junior Undiscovered Math Prodigies). My goal at the time was rather modest. I knew, from my own experience, how easily children could become convinced they were incapable of doing well in mathematics. I wanted to give free, private tutoring in the subject to elementary students from working families in my neighbourhood.

Since its inception in my apartment, with 8 tutors and 15 students, JUMP has grown exponentially; it is now established in 12 inner-city schools in Toronto, with over 200 volunteers and 1,500 students. I expect the program will continue to grow at this pace, in part because the volunteers are not required to have any background in mathematics. Several of our best instructors dropped out of mathematics in high school. Working from a manual I developed for the program, tutors relearn the subject properly as they teach.

Six units from *The JUMP Teaching Manual* are included in Part 2 of this book. These units illustrate fully the teaching method used in JUMP. The method is easily learned and becomes automatic with practice. Teachers who work through these units with students should see very quickly how they can adapt the approach to teaching any kind of mathematics.

In many of the units in the manual (as illustrated in the fractions unit, Chapter 6), new concepts and operations are introduced in extremely mechanical steps that a student cannot fail to grasp. While the steps are simple, the goal of the JUMP method is not to produce students who can do math only by rote. In some units, students are taught to solve problems requiring careful reasoning and systematic search; in others, topics normally covered in high school or university are introduced. (Two enriched units are included in Chapters 10 and 11 of this book.)

The manual assumes that young children are capable of understanding advanced mathematics, but it does not ask students who have fallen behind to struggle with open-ended problems without guidance, as do many of the texts now used in schools. Even in the most advanced units of the manual, students are taught how to find solutions by first working on simplified models of a problem.

Over the past four years, I have observed a great many remarkable leaps in intelligence and ability in students taught mathematics using the method described in this book. My first student, who was in a remedial class in Grade 6 and couldn't count by twos, is now in a Grade 10 academic program a year ahead of her grade level. And in several elementary classes where JUMP was tested, all of the students, including many who were thought to be slow learners, incapable of concentrating or learning advanced mathematics, scored over 80% on a Grade 6–7 fractions test after less than two months of instruction. To my knowledge, results of this sort have not been documented in our schools.

There are several reasons why such dramatic improvements in mathematical ability, particularly among remedial students, have not been observed in the school system. Most people who are good at mathematics develop a talent for the subject when they are quite young. As adults, they are scarcely conscious of the steps they follow in solving problems. Consequently, they may find it hard to isolate or describe those steps and will often blame students for their own failings as teachers.

Because I had struggled with mathematics myself, I was inclined when I started JUMP to observe my students carefully to see why they were failing. I didn't have to look far. I examined a book of sample problems in mathematics used in Ontario's schools. Though the book was intended for teachers, there was almost no discussion of how to guide a student, step by step, to understand and solve the problems. The book was a catalogue of failure: it described, in meticulous detail, all of the incomplete and erroneous answers a teacher might expect from students and suggested a mark for each answer. This approach did not strike me as unusual: I've never seen a text among the many teachers' guides I've read that consistently introduces mathematical concepts in an order any student could grasp, or that lays out the steps of an explanation in a way that any teacher could communicate. I have seen guides filled with excellent exercises and activities, but none aimed at closing the gap between the weakest and strongest students. Books that purport to teach teachers often seem more concerned with classifying students: one learns how to label children according to learning styles or disabilities, but not how to deliver a lesson that will be understood by every child in a class of 25.

Apart from the lack of effective texts (and inadequate training for teachers), there is, I believe, a more fundamental reason why dramatic improvements in mathematical ability have not been observed in our schools. Until recently, a theory that even allowed for these improvements did not exist. Most models of learning assume that intelligence and mathematical ability are fixed: by reducing explanations to trivial steps, one can add only tiny increments to a student's knowledge. Slower children will become a little better at math, but only by parroting what they have learned by rote. The results of JUMP appear to contradict this expectation. In Chapter 2 of this book, I will argue that a new branch of mathematics, chaos theory, may account for the non-linear leaps in ability that have been observed in JUMP students. I will also call into question a number of universally held beliefs about mathematical ability.

Based on my work with elementary students, I am now convinced that all children, except possibly those who are so severely disabled that they would not be enrolled in a regular public school, can be led to think mathematically. (I say "possibly" because I have not worked with children who are outside the regular school system: it wouldn't surprise me if these children were capable of more than people expect.) Even if I am wrong, the results of JUMP suggest that it is worth suspending judgement in individual cases. A teacher who expects a student to fail is almost certain to produce a failure. The method of teaching outlined in this book (or any method, for that matter) is more likely to succeed if it is applied with patience and an open mind.

PART 1

How JUMP Started

CHAPTER 1

A Series of Fortunate Events

W HEN I WAS QUITE YOUNG, I BELIEVE NO OLDER THAN 11, I came across two books that would determine how I thought about mathematics for the next 20 years, until, at the age of 31, I found the confidence to return to school and start a degree in the subject. One book was a collection of science fiction from the local library. It contained a story about two children who construct a Möbius strip that enables them, by a process I unfortunately can't recall, to travel in time. The other book belonged to my older sister, who was studying psychology at the time. It was a thick book, full of charts and formulas, on giftedness in children.

Though I haven't reread the short story since I was a child, I would be surprised if it was well written, and even more surprised if the mathematics behind it was sound. But the story awoke a greater sense of wonder than I have felt reading anything since: from it I gained the conviction that mathematics was a magical subject that would allow me, once I had mastered it, to transcend the everyday.

My sister's book was less inspiring. I found the charts and formulas impossible to decipher, but I knew from the introduction what they implied: that I would become a mathematician only if I had inherited a gift for the subject.

The moment I learned that I couldn't simply decide to become a mathematician, I began to reflect on my early childhood to see if I was lucky enough to have been born a prodigy. I read biographies of successful scientists and mathematicians so I could compare my development with theirs. I recall one book, *The Mind*, quite clearly. It contained a painting of two dozen geniuses, with an intelligence quotient printed beside each one. Gauss, a mathematician, had scored much higher than the rest, in part because he'd discovered a trick for summing the numbers from one to 100 when he was only eight.

It seemed clear, from everything I read, that a person born to do mathematics would never do badly on a test or struggle to learn a new concept. The thoughts and mental processes of a great scientist or mathematician were of an order entirely different from those of an ordinary person. As this belief sank in, I began to find math more difficult at school and my marks steadily declined. When I received a D (later belled to a C) in Calculus for the Life Sciences at university, I decided to drop the subject once and for all.

One evening, a year after I had finished my undergraduate studies, I began reading a book of letters by the poet Sylvia Plath, which I'd found on my sister's bookshelf while babysitting her children. (I still hadn't learned how dangerous it was to read my sister's books.) As a child, I loved writing as much as I loved mathematics, but in this, too, I had shown few signs of innate talent. Though I received a B in creative writing at university, it was the lowest mark given in the class.

It appeared from Plath's letters and early poems that she had taught herself to write by sheer determination. She had learned, as a teenager, everything she could about poetic meter and form. She wrote sonnets and sestinas, memorized the thesaurus, and read mythology. She also produced dozens of imitations of poems she admired.

Even with Plath's example to guide me, I wasn't entirely certain I could choose to develop a skill for something I loved. But I resolved to try to teach myself to write the way she had. Ten years later, I received a Governor General's Award for my work as a playwright.

Awards do not necessarily certify that an artist's work is good, but they do at least indicate basic competence.

As I found it impossible to make a living as a playwright (the $10,000 award increased my cumulative earnings in theatre by about 300%), I supported myself with a series of part-time jobs. One day, when I was 28, I answered a notice at a placement centre for a math tutor. I had become interested in math again after helping a friend who was returning to school with a problem in calculus. Reading her textbook slowly and carefully, without the pressure of having to study for exams, I found the material much easier than I had at university. I convinced the woman who ran the tutorial agency that I could teach math because I had passed a course in calculus (she wasn't aware of my mark) along with several courses in logic.

One of my first students was close to failing Grade 8 math. He had been told by his teacher that he wasn't bright enough to do well in the subject. Having struggled with math myself, I decided to observe the boy carefully before I made any judgements about his ability. He proved to be an ideal student. He worked hard and soon developed an interest in mathematics. Because I hadn't assumed that he lacked ability, and because I was lucky enough to work with him for a period of five years, I saw changes in his aptitude that few teachers ever see in their students. In Grade 13, my student did so well in the Sir Isaac Newton physics competition, he was offered a scholarship to Waterloo University, even though he hadn't applied there. He is presently completing a doctorate in mathematics at another university.

Seeing how quickly several of my students were developing as mathematicians, I began to think about my own progress in the subject. Because I made an effort, in my tutorials, to reduce explanations to simple steps, many of the concepts and operations that had seemed mysterious in high school were becoming clear. It now seemed possible, by teaching myself mathematics the way I had taught myself to write, that I might realize my childhood dream of being a mathematician. I enrolled in two first-year mathematics courses at a local university.

When I received the results of my first test, I wasn't surprised to see that I had failed. I knew the test wasn't fair: some of the material had not been covered in class (it was taught several weeks later). As the professor handed back the tests, he read out the names of the few people who had passed and told the rest of us that we should consider dropping the course. Many students did exactly that; the ones I talked to believed that the professor had made an objective assessment of their prospects as mathematicians. I stayed in the course, but only because of the confidence I had gained as a tutor.

I failed other tests from time to time, in other courses, including two of three comprehensive exams for my doctorate. In the beginning, it was very hard to suppress the feeling that I had failed because I had finally reached a level of mathematics that was beyond me. Gradually I saw that questions I once found impossible on a particular test seemed trivial a month or a year later: there was no threshold that separated one level of mathematics from another. Sometimes I did badly because I was nervous (on my comprehensives I made mistakes that were equivalent, in higher mathematics, to $2 + 2 = 5$) or because I hadn't had time to digest the material properly. Sometimes the tests were unfair.

Unfortunately, few of the students who enrolled in mathematics the year I did survived long enough to gain the confidence and background they needed to do well and to overlook an occasional failure. Several of the professors seemed more intent on weeding people out than on teaching them: by fourth year, only eight of the hundred or so students who started were still in the department.

When I was growing up, my parents would billet students from Africa so they could go to our local university. My father often worked for free as a surgeon in hospitals in Africa, and my mother helped administer and raise funds for several Third World charities. By the time I had returned to university, I began to feel that I hadn't really lived up to their example. Even after winning the Governor General's Award, I wasn't sure my writing amounted to much more than a self-indulgence. I searched several community papers until I found a volunteer program that was looking for tutors.

The program, which was listed under the Canadian Alliance of Black School Teachers, was run by two saintly teachers, Ken and Inez Johnson, who had spent years doing volunteer teaching and advocacy work for inner-city kids, and who didn't seem to mind the fact that I wasn't black. They assigned me to a Saturday morning homework club, where I tutored math, mainly to high-school students.

The Saturday sessions were very successful (I continued teaching there even after I started JUMP), but I was frustrated by one aspect of the classes. Some of the students would make spectacular progress for a lesson or two, then not show up again for a month. Though I was proud of the students who came every week and did well at school, I thought more often about the ones who were never there. I had the feeling, with those students, that I was bailing out a lifeboat. I knew the boat would sink eventually, and I could do nothing to prevent it.

For several years I thought about starting a program for elementary students. I assumed they would be less likely than high-school students to have given up on school. There were two spare rooms in my apartment, which, in addition to my kitchen, would make adequate classrooms. Inez had been vice-principal of a school a short walk from my apartment. She convinced the principal, Silvana Carletti, to select 15 children for tutoring. Several of my friends were brave enough to volunteer as tutors, even though they had never taught math. Half an hour before the first students arrived, I reminded the tutors how to add fractions. Beyond that, I wasn't sure what we were going to teach the kids. I was, however, full of optimism: I had already decided to call the program Junior Undiscovered Math Prodigies — or JUMP.

After five minutes with my first student, I was certain the whole enterprise would be a terrible disaster. I had asked Silvana to send students in Grades 4 or 5, but the girl who sat down at my table looked older. When I asked what she had learned about fractions at school, she said, "Nothing." I said she would find them very easy, but first I needed to know if there were any times tables she had trouble remembering. She looked at me with a blank expression. She had no idea what multiplication meant. Even the concept of counting by a number other than one was foreign to her: she was not able to count by twos. Silvana had assumed, when I asked for children who were struggling in math, that I'd wanted students in remedial classes. Lisa was in Grade 6, but knew less mathematics than a typical child in Grade 1. She was terrified by my questions and kept saying, when I mentioned the simplest concepts, "I don't understand." She also had trouble reading and told me she had never read a chapter book in her life.

I had promised a lesson in fractions, and as I had no idea what else to do, I began counting slowly on my fingers by twos, asking Lisa if she could do the same. I wasn't certain she would ever understand the concept of fractions but wanted at least to see if she could carry out basic operations, changing the denominators of simple fractions by multiplying on her fingers. Lisa made several attempts to count to 10 by twos but couldn't remember the correct sequence of numbers. As she was clearly growing more nervous with each failure, I told her she was brilliant, even though she could only repeat the sequence up to six. The encouragement helped her focus, and by the end of the lesson she had made more progress than I expected. The next day, her mother told me Lisa had had a nightmare that she wouldn't be allowed to return to tutorials. I was the first teacher who had ever told her she was smart.

Lisa has been in JUMP for three years now. I find it hard to believe that she ever had trouble mastering simple mathematics. Her rate of learning seems to double by the week: lately she has even started teaching herself new material from a textbook when I'm not available to answer her questions. Lisa recently moved from a remedial class (where she was still being taught the most basic math) into a regular Grade 9 academic class. Several weeks ago I also found out that she'd enrolled, of her own volition, in Grade 10 math for the next semester. Soon Lisa will be a year ahead of her grade level.

Though I had asked Lisa's mother to place her in an academic math program, I began to have misgivings during the first week of class. There were still large gaps in Lisa's background I felt would be difficult to fill in, particularly in a semester course. A teacher at the high school called Lisa's mother several times to ask why Lisa had been placed in an academic class. She even told Lisa directly that she should move to a basic class. According to the school's records, Lisa was still at an elementary level; on top of that she had failed her first test. But Lisa, who previously had been terrified of teachers, refused to leave the class. When she received a 90% on her second test, I breathed a sigh of relief. Since then, Lisa has learned an enormous amount of new material, including much that her peers have been working on for years. Though there are still large gaps in her background (her marks oscillate wildly between 40% and 100%, with most falling in the C to B range), I am certain she will pass her course.

Lisa is not an isolated case. Three of the four oldest students in JUMP moved from remedial classes to academic Grade 9 classes recently. (The mother of the fourth student was convinced by a teacher that her daughter would not be able to handle academic math.) As well, many of the younger students in JUMP have made remarkable progress, which I describe in more detail in Chapters 2 and 4.

Lisa advanced from a Grade 1 to a Grade 9 level after only a hundred hours of tutorials (fewer lessons than she would have received in a single year of school). I am certain she would have progressed much further if I had been less quick to judge her and more adept at presenting advanced material. The students in JUMP have taught me how little I knew about teaching. The main principles of the program were thrust upon me, in embryonic form, even in the first lessons. The students Silvana had selected were so delayed that I was forced, as I had never been with previous students, to reduce mathematics to steps no one could fail to grasp. Just to keep them going, I was compelled to tell students who appeared unteachable that they were smart, only to realize later what I'd said in fact was true.

It can take an hour to convince a child he or she is intelligent; with an adult, sadly, it could take forever. Recently I told a teacher of enriched mathematics about the remarkable changes I'd observed in children enrolled in JUMP. I was responding to his claim that real mathematical ability can never be nurtured, because it is genetically determined. He said that though I was smarter than he (because I had gone further in mathematics), he had more experience with kids. I never questioned his experience (though it had been solely with teenagers who had already suffered at least nine years in the public school system), but I found his lack of confidence telling: he easily might have gone further himself if he hadn't been prevented by his beliefs.

I sometimes wish I could travel back to my childhood to regain the time I wasted in self-doubt (and not just in mathematics). But I'm grateful to have found some faith in my abilities. One day, I hope that same faith will be considered the right of all children, and they will not have to wait for some accident, like a book of letters, or a tutor assigned by mistake, to reveal the vast potential that might otherwise have been lost.

CHAPTER 2

Myths about Math

TWO OF THE FIRST JUMP STUDENTS, ANA AND MARGARET, FOUND it hard to concentrate for more than several minutes at a time when they started the program. Both girls were in Grade 6, but neither could consistently add a pair of single-digit numbers, even using their fingers. After several months of lessons they were making progress, adding and manipulating simple fractions. One day, while I was busy helping another JUMP student, Ana began leafing through a Grade 7 text she'd picked up from my table. When I turned to work with her, she handed me a sheet of paper on which she'd added some fractions. It was the answer to a word problem from the book. The problem was harder than anything I'd covered in my lessons thus far, and Ana had solved it without my help. Several months later, I gave Margaret a sheet of paired ratios with a term missing in each pair. Normally, I teach students to find the missing term in cases where they must multiply before I show them how to find the missing term by dividing. On Margaret's sheet, I had mixed up the two kinds of questions. While I was busy thinking about how I would teach her to distinguish between the two cases, she answered the questions correctly without hesitation.

Even though Ana and Margaret had learned to work with

fractions much more quickly than I had expected, these new displays of ability seemed almost uncanny. Both girls had been placed in classes for severely learning-disabled children: they were years behind even the students I had taught who were failing regular classes. With my help, they had learned how to manipulate fractions, but only by following a sequence of small, mechanical steps. Now, it seemed, they'd been able to teach themselves mathematical concepts without any assistance. New abilities had emerged, suddenly and mysteriously, from entirely mechanical work.

Not long ago, in the 1960s, mathematicians and scientists began to notice a property of natural systems that had been overlooked since the dawn of science: that tiny changes of condition, even in stable systems, can have dramatic and often unpredictable effects. From stock markets to storm fronts, systems of any significant degree of complexity exhibit non-linear or chaotic behaviour. For example, if one adds a reagent, one drop at a time, to a chemical solution, nothing may happen at all until, with the addition of a single drop, the whole mixture changes colour. And, as a saying made current by chaos theory goes, if a butterfly flaps its wings over the ocean, it can change the weather over New York.

As the brain is an immensely complicated organ, made up of billions of neurons, it would be surprising if it did not exhibit chaotic behaviour, even in its higher mental functions. Like the chemical solution that changes colour after one last drop of reagent, Ana and Margaret's new abilities emerged suddenly and dramatically from a series of small conceptual advances. I have witnessed the same progression in dozens of students: a surprising leap forward, followed by a period where the student appears to have reached the limits of their abilities; then another tiny advance that precipitates another leap. One of my students, who was in a remedial Grade 5 class when he started JUMP, progressed so quickly that by Grade 7 he received a mark of 91% in a regular class (and his teacher told his mother he was now the smartest kid in the class). And Lisa, who couldn't count by twos in Grade 6, now teaches herself new material from a difficult academic Grade 9 text.

If non-linear leaps in intelligence and ability are possible, as the results of the JUMP program suggest, why haven't these effects been observed in our schools? I believe the answer lies in the profound inertia of human thought: when an entire society believes something is impossible, it suppresses, by its very way of life, the evidence that would contradict that belief. History provides ample proof of the blindness we display when observing ourselves. Only 50 years ago, everyone believed that women and people with dark skin were intellectually inferior to males with white skin. Unfortunately, this kind of prejudice still underlies most of our thinking about intellectual (and even artistic) ability.

Biologists tend to attribute differences in behaviour among animals of the same species to differences in material condition, and they test their hypotheses rigorously by varying those conditions. But ask the biologists themselves if they are gifted in mathematics and they will almost certainly reply, "I don't have that kind of brain," just as an artist might say, "I'm more of a right-brain person." Twelve or 13 years in oversized classes, in a system predicated on the idea that only a few students will excel: these factors are not considered to be complicit in the problem. Failure in this system stands as irrefutable proof, even for the person failing, that one was born not to succeed.

Most people can recall a classmate in grade school who never seemed to work but always did well on tests. The fact that mathematical ability appears spontaneously in a gifted child is cited as evidence that ability is determined by genetics. But if the mind, like other complex systems, is subject to chaotic and non-linear effects, even siblings with the same genetic features, and who are offered the same opportunities, might develop entirely different abilities. Some small event in early childhood or at school might start an avalanche of learning in one child but not another. The fact that an avalanche occurs on one mountain and not another does not imply anything interesting about mountains. It does not prove that one mountain is more prone to avalanches or that an avalanche could never be started.

People who claim that they were born without mathematical ability will often admit that they were good at the subject until a certain grade, as though the gene for mathematics carried a definite expiry date. Most people will also recall an unusual coincidence: that the year their ability disappeared, they had a particularly bad teacher.

Prior to the 20th century, in cultures where women were discouraged from studying mathematics, half the human population produced only a handful of mathematicians. No experiment could demonstrate more conclusively how a universally held belief becomes self-fulfilling.

Perhaps more than in any other subject, in mathematics it is easy to turn a good student into a bad one in a very short time. The myths surrounding the subject encourage children to give up the moment they encounter any difficulty. As well, mathematical knowledge is cumulative: a child who misses a step in the development of a concept cannot go on.

I conducted a rudimentary experiment with a Grade 3 class recently to see how much they could learn in a month if they were taught by the JUMP method, with adequate tutorial support. I gave four weeks of lessons (each lesson 40 minutes long) on fractions, followed by a week of review. Two volunteer tutors came into the class once a week, and the teacher assisted in most lessons. Five students, including three who were considered learning disabled or slow learners, received three extra tutorials in groups of two or three students. (The details of the experiment are given in Chapter 4.)

At the end of five weeks the class wrote a practice test, followed, the next day, by a 15-minute review, then a final. On both tests the children were expected to name fractions, add and subtract fractions, reduce fractions, change mixed fractions to improper fractions (and vice versa), add mixed fractions, compare fractions for size, and solve simple word problems involving fractions. Because at least half of the class didn't know any times tables when I started the lessons, the denominators in most of the questions on the tests were divisible by two, three, four, or five (the children had learned how to multiply and divide by these numbers over the course of the month). Otherwise the tests were at a solid Grade 6–7 level. (The final test is reproduced on page 113.)

All of the students in the class scored over 80% on the practice test and over 90% on the final (with more than half of them scoring 100% on the final). By the time they wrote the tests, the weakest students in the class had shown remarkable improvements in concentration, memory, and numerical ability, so that there was much less of a gap between them and the strongest students. One boy, who had been recommended for a slow-learners class, finished his practice test ahead of half the class and scored 90%. (He took more time on his final, but still scored 92%.) The children were thrilled to be doing challenging mathematics because they knew they would not be allowed to fail. When I said to the class, "You all got As on the practice test — do you think I need to give you the final?" the students shouted in unison, "Yes!"

Based on my observations of hundreds of students, I predict that with proper teaching and minimal tutorial support, a Grade 3 class could easily reach a Grade 6 or 7 level in all areas of the mathematics curriculum without a single student being left behind. Imagine how far children might go (and how much they might enjoy learning) if they were offered this kind of support throughout their school years. It is possible, of course, that children who had a head start in early childhood might always remain ahead of their peers (although I believe that significant differences between children would tend to disappear if the children were all offered proper support in the lower grades). It is even possible, though I do not personally believe this, that some children might be genetically programmed to be more intelligent than others. But even if this were the case, it would not, I expect, be of any consequence in a society that educated its children. This is where the debate about intelligence misses the point. The results of JUMP suggest that we can raise the level of even the weakest students sufficiently to enable them to appreciate and master genuine mathematics. At this level, sheer intelligence is almost secondary. In the sciences, factors such as passion, confidence, creativity, diligence, luck, and artistic flair are as important as the speed and sharpness of one's mind. Einstein was not a great mathematician technically, but he had a deep sense of beauty and a willingness to question conventional wisdom.

If a music teacher were to say, "Gifted children will simply pick up an instrument and play well; the rest will only become mediocre musicians," we would take it as a sign of incompetence. Why, then, do we tolerate this view among teachers of mathematics? Why are our schools satisfied if only one-fifth of their students demonstrate a mastery of the curriculum? And why are most mathematics classes so large that only a few students could ever hope to ask a question and have it answered?

A simple analogy shows the extent to which people still believe that only a few children are born with intellectual ability. If children in any part of Canada were being starved to the point where they looked like famine victims, people would demand that they be fed. But children regularly graduate from our schools after reaching only a tiny fraction of their potential. Why do we tolerate this vast loss of potential, this great neglect of our children? It is not because we are inhuman. We must all believe, on some level, that these children are not being starved, they are simply incapable of eating.

Positive social change only occurs when enough people recognize something as unfair. Apathy alone does not stop people from acting: we tolerate suffering or injustice because we have failed to see something that seems obvious once it is understood (witness the treatment of people of colour in North America). What would happen if we devoted as much effort to teaching students as we do to assessing them and proving them different? The weakest students would likely surpass the standards now set for the strongest. As long as we insist that mathematicians are born and not made, we will tolerate poorly designed programs in our schools and classrooms in which children who have fallen behind cannot get the help they need to succeed.

CHAPTER 3

Copying, Counting, and Comparing

In the grade 3 class where I taught for a month, one of the boys would peer into his desk from time to time when he thought no one was looking. If I was standing directly behind him, I would bend my knees slightly so I could follow his line of sight, but I never was able to see what he found so fascinating about the interior of his desk. To me, it appeared to be full of books and pencils.

Teachers often forget the gulf that separates them from their students. I dimly remember living in a world where anything was possible, but even if I tried my hardest now, I doubt I could find anything magical in the shadows of an ordinary desk.

When we make assessments of children, we expect them to see the world as we do. But their way of perceiving things is almost unimaginably different from ours. In teaching mathematics, we shouldn't judge young students too quickly for failing to apply a rule correctly, even after we have shown them a number of examples. Children can be very creative in extending rules to cases they have never seen. A child who learns to apply a rule using small numbers will often believe the rule changes or stops working beyond a certain point, as if a number could grow so enormous it caused things to break. Many rules are also counterintuitive in ways that may not be obvious to an adult. In adding two halves of separate pies, for example, one still has four pieces between the two pies; why then, a child might wonder, isn't the denominator in the final fraction four?

Learning mathematics, even at the highest levels, is often a matter of getting used to things: there are concepts that only become clear after a great deal of use. A few examples may not be enough to show a child, whose understanding has not been conditioned by years of experience, how to extend a rule to a potentially infinite number of cases. Even the simplest instructions can be ambiguous to a student who is still learning to distinguish shadows from monsters.

All of the books of elementary mathematics I have read recently seem to expect children to master concepts and operations with very little practice, after being shown only a few (or often no) examples. Several weeks ago, I found an exercise in a Grade 3 book that asked students, in each question, to shade a given fraction of an array of boxes. In most of the questions the number of boxes in the array matched the denominator of the fraction, so the student simply had to look at the numerator of the fraction and shade that many boxes. But halfway through the exercise there was an array of 20 boxes with the instruction "Shade one-fifth of the boxes." Up to that point students had not been taught anything about equivalent fractions, or even how to divide a number into equal parts.

Open almost any current book of elementary mathematics to any page and you are likely to find an example of the sort of conceptual leap I found in that Grade 3 book. The majority of teachers are not trained to fill in such gaps. Nor do they have the time, while supervising and preparing lessons for upwards of 25 children, to rewrite the material they are required to teach.

I was asked by a journalist recently what I thought of the "new math," a method of teaching now prevalent in Canadian schools in which students solve open-ended problems by discussing and writing down explanations of their work. In the piece she wrote, the journalist made it sound as if I'd advocated a return to more traditional forms of instruction based largely on drills and rote learning. But I had been careful to stress to her that the ideals of the new math were not in themselves responsible for making many children feel incapable of doing mathematics. Rather, it was the *way* those ideals have been implemented in our schools — with textbooks that appear to have been written in a great hurry and by teachers who have received insufficient training and support — that has caused the current crisis in elementary education.

In the second year of JUMP, I began writing a manual for the program's tutors. The program had grown from seven to 15 tutors, so I could no longer meet with tutors individually to explain how to teach a particular topic. Before this time, it had never occurred to me to write down the steps I followed in explaining various concepts. As with most of the innovations in JUMP, the idea of producing a set of lesson plans was forced on me by sheer necessity.

The manual is still a work in progress: I constantly test units on my students and make improvements based on their responses. I also rely on tutors to tell me when the units are unclear or difficult to implement. Lately I have added material to bring the manual into line with the curriculum of Ontario, so teachers can use it in the classroom.

In hindsight, I can see it was fortunate that I had planned to teach fractions in my first JUMP lesson. Most programs for remedial students consist of endless drills in addition and multiplication. Because children in special classes are assumed to be intellectually challenged, they gradually lose all confidence and motivation, so that after several years of extra help in math they can scarcely retain even the simplest facts. Many of the students who enter the JUMP program have not, after five or six years of regular school, managed to learn even the three-times table. Based on four years of work with these students, I have come to believe the best way to motivate children who have fallen behind is to skip them ahead — to convince them they are capable of doing work beyond their grade level. JUMP students who complete the first unit of the book are expected to write a test on fractions at a Grade 6–7 level, and they must score 80% or higher to go on to the next unit. Most students accomplish this in three or four months of weekly lessons. Very few need to take the test twice.

The JUMP program was specifically developed to help children who have fallen behind catch up quickly. I would never claim it is the only way to teach mathematics, or even the best. Programs based more on manipulatives, or that introduce concepts in an order different from the order in the manual, might work as well or better. I would claim, however, that whatever method is used, the teacher should never assume that a student who initially fails to understand an explanation is therefore incapable of progressing.

A tutor once told me that one of her students, a girl in Grade 4, had refused to let her teach her how to divide. The girl said that the concept of division was much too hard for her and she would never consent to learn it. I suggested that the tutor teach division as a kind of counting game. In the next lesson, without telling the girl she was about to learn how to divide, the tutor wrote in succession the numbers 15 and 5. Then she asked the child to count on her fingers by multiples of the second number, until she'd reached the first. After the child had repeated this operation with several other pairs of numbers, the tutor asked her to write down, in each case, the number of fingers she had raised when she stopped counting. For instance,

15   5   <u>3</u>

As soon as the student could find the answer to any such question quickly, the tutor wrote, in each example, a division sign between the first and second number, and an equal sign between the second and third.

15 ÷ 5 = 3

The student was surprised to find she had learned to divide in 10 minutes. (Of course, the tutor later explained to her that 15 divided by 5 is 3 because you can add 5 three times to get 15: that's what you see when you count on your fingers.)

Any child in Grade 3 or 4, in a regular school, is able to erase or cross out a letter or numeral, or copy a letter or numeral from one part of a page to another. The child is also able, given two numbers between 0 and 9, to say which one is larger than the other. Finally, with a little practice, any child should be able to count, on the fingers of one hand, by ones, twos, and threes (and eventually by higher numbers). These are the only skills children need to have mastered, along with basic addition and subtraction (even if it's only on their fingers), to carry out the operations in the JUMP manual.

Students in JUMP are always allowed to master the simplest instances of an operation before they are taught the more complicated ones. Two numbers are relatively prime if their lowest common multiple (the lowest number they both divide into evenly) is their product. For instance, 2 and 3 are relatively prime, but 4 and 6 are not (since the product of 4 and 6 is 24, while their lowest common multiple is 12). To add two fractions with relatively prime denominators the student must simply multiply the top and bottom of each fraction by the denominator of the other. (The reason for this is explained in the fractions unit; see Chapter 6.) For instance:

$$\frac{1}{2} + \frac{1}{3} \longrightarrow \frac{3 \times 1}{3 \times 2} + \frac{1 \times 2}{3 \times 2}$$

As this is simply a matter of copying numbers from one place on the page to another, any students can carry out this operation, even if they don't fully understand the concept underlying it. Some students, however, may have very poor memories and visual skills when they start the program: even copying the right numbers in the right places may be a challenge. Several of my students were thrown off if I changed the position of the answer on the page — if I wrote, for instance:

$$\frac{1}{2} + \frac{1}{3}$$

$$= \frac{3 \times 1}{3 \times 2} + \frac{1 \times 2}{3 \times 2}$$

and then wrote:

$$\frac{1}{3} + \frac{1}{5} = \frac{5 \times 1}{5 \times 3} + \frac{1 \times 3}{5 \times 3}$$

It is always possible, however, even with the weakest student, to make it easier for the student to proceed. You might, for instance, write in the times signs for the student:

$$\frac{1}{2} + \frac{1}{3} \longrightarrow \frac{\times 1}{\times 2} + \frac{1 \times}{3 \times}$$

so the student simply has to put the right numbers in the right places:

$$\frac{\times 1}{\times 2} + \frac{1 \times}{3 \times} \longrightarrow \frac{3 \times 1}{3 \times 2} + \frac{1 \times 2}{3 \times 2}$$

Or you might have them transfer only one symbol at a time:

$$\frac{1}{2} + \frac{1}{3} \longrightarrow \frac{\bigcirc \times 1}{\bigcirc \times 2} + \frac{1}{3} \longrightarrow \frac{3 \times 1}{3 \times 2} + \frac{1}{3}$$

$$\longrightarrow \frac{3 \times 1}{3 \times 2} + \frac{1 \times}{3 \times} \frac{\bigcirc}{\bigcirc} \longrightarrow \frac{3 \times 1}{3 \times 2} + \frac{1 \times 2}{3 \times 2}$$

drawing the circles to help them place the numbers. All of the steps in this manual can be simplified in this way. If a student gets stuck, you can always look for a way to make the step easier.

Once students learn a step, it is important to allow them to repeat it until they have mastered it. When I teach a step I give several examples and then write out two or three questions, leaving enough room under each question for the students to work. After several tests of this sort, when I am sure the students can reproduce the step automatically, I move on to the next step. When they have mastered all of the steps, I give them several tests where they must perform the operation completely. I usually end each lesson with a test that reviews everything we've covered.

Of course, it may seem like basic common sense to teach one step at a time, but even an experienced teacher will often compress a number of steps into one without realizing it. In adding fractions with relatively prime denominators, one performs the following steps:

$$\frac{1}{2} + \frac{1}{3} = \quad \textbf{Step 1:} \quad \frac{3 \times 1}{3 \times 2} + \frac{1 \times 2}{3 \times 2}$$

$$\textbf{Step 2:} \quad \frac{3}{6} + \frac{2}{6}$$

$$\textbf{Step 3:} \quad \frac{5}{6}$$

If you teach all three steps at once, a weaker student will not be able to remember the first step by the time you have reached the last. You may well waste a whole lesson and leave the student demoralized, having learned nothing. If, however, you proceed one step at a time, allowing time for repetition, you can teach the weakest student to perform this operation in half a lesson.

Students should never be expected, when learning a new operation, to employ knowledge or a skill that they haven't mastered. It would be unwise, for instance, to teach a student who has a shaky grasp of the six-times table to add fractions by producing examples with denominators divisible by six. The strain of trying to recall the six-times table could only interfere with the student's ability to remember the steps.

While this might seem like an obvious principle, it is, I believe, regularly ignored in the schools. Students in JUMP are taught first to count on their fingers by twos, threes, and fives (which they quickly master). All operations taught in the first unit are introduced with fractions whose denominators are divisible by those numbers.

In explaining elementary mathematics, it is all too easy to introduce concepts that are beyond a student's level of understanding. A JUMP tutor once told a beginning student that the fraction $\frac{4}{4}$ was equal to 1 because 4 "goes into itself" once. The tutor then wrote "10,000/10,000 = ___ " and asked the student to fill in the answer. As the student had no real familiarity with the concept of division, she had no idea what "goes into" meant. She just saw the huge numbers and panicked. (The tutor had to spend half a lesson rebuilding the student's confidence.)

The problem of reducing fractions like $\frac{4}{4}$ to whole numbers can be turned into an entirely mechanical procedure. For instance, students might simply write the word "same" beside a fraction in which the numerator and denominator are the same, and then write "= 1" in cases where they have written "same." Similarly, the concept of a number "going into" another can be introduced as a mechanical procedure (counting on your fingers by the first number and checking to see if you ever say the second).

In developing the JUMP manual, I was surprised to see the extent to which mathematics can be reduced to pre-conceptual operations like counting, crossing out a number or symbol, moving a number or symbol from one place on a page to another place, and so on. The fractions unit and the ratios and percents unit in this book were written to illustrate how far this approach can be taken (see Chapters 6 and 7). In working with weaker students, a teacher can always break an operation into steps the student cannot fail to perform. This style of teaching need not be followed indefinitely; even the most delayed student, in my experience, will eventually begin to skip steps and deduce explanations for themselves. But unless teachers begin with extremely simple tasks, they are not likely to help the majority of their students.

As far as I am aware, no program in mathematics was ever developed with the expectation that every child in the program would excel. To most educators, the idea of an entire class doing well in any subject seems absurd. A teacher who gave out only As would soon be called before the principal. Even in the present curriculum, which demands relatively little of students, no one would believe such marks were legitimate.

In working with the students in JUMP, I have come to understand why so many children have trouble learning mathematics. Our schools fail to produce, in the majority of children, skills and attitudes that are essential to abstract thought. Teachers who neglect to develop these basic capacities in their students do not have a hope of succeeding with their whole class.

Before children are introduced to mathematical concepts, they must, above all, be confident they will not be allowed to fail. They must be attentive and excited about learning. They must be able to recognize simple patterns in numbers and be capable of making elementary deductions — deciding, for instance, when to use one algorithm rather than another to carry out an operation. They must be able to follow basic rules and have some idea of what it means to extend a rule to a new case. Finally, they must be able to concentrate long enough to carry out operations of several steps and manipulate numbers well enough to carry out each step without hesitation.

The fractions unit in Chapter 6 of this book is designed to build the skills and attitudes a student needs to learn genuine mathematics. While the steps in every exercise are easy to follow (so that even the weakest student need never be discouraged), the conceptual work inherent in the unit is far from trivial. The goal of even the most mechanical exercises is to prepare a student for more advanced mathematics.

I am convinced, after observing a great many delayed students, that the problems these students face often stem from the same source. Students who have struggled with math for a number of years will likely have developed a kind of guessing mechanism that serves them well at school. No matter what you are teaching, even if it is quite simple, they probably won't have a clue what you are saying. They will try to get a vague sense of your meaning, while most of their attention is being diverted to formulating a good guess. The method of teaching followed in the fractions unit is very effective at breaking such habits. If students are always able to carry out a given step, they soon develop a faith that they can understand anything the teacher expects them to learn. The startling improvements I have seen in my students are, I believe, largely due to one cause: for the first time these students have been given enough confidence to listen.

Nothing focuses the attention of children more sharply than the feeling that they are meeting a series of challenges and succeeding brilliantly. When adding fractions with different denominators, JUMP students will first count by the smaller denominator, checking to see whether they reach the larger. In this way, by repeatedly adding fractions, the students quickly learn how to divide. A fact learned while practising challenging mathematics is more readily recalled than one learned by rote drill. In JUMP, students who required four years to memorize a single times table at school become capable, in four months, of manipulating fractions at a Grade 7 level. The rapid progress made by our students shows the enormous role a student's perception plays in learning. Clearly, students learn more quickly if they feel they are doing advanced work and succeeding.

By the time students complete section F-6 in the fractions unit of the manual, they will know how to add fractions in the following cases: when the denominators of the fractions are the same; when one denominator divides the other; and when the denominators are relatively prime. By learning to distinguish between these cases, these students will have taken a significant first step in their conceptual development: they will have learned how to choose between one of a set of algorithms for carrying out an extended sequence of logical or computational steps. While the students' understanding of fractions will still be quite rudimentary, the effect of their growing mechanical facility often can be quite dramatic. I have observed marked improvements in memory, concentration, and numerical ability in many students after only a month of tutoring (see Chapter 4).

In the fractions unit, students are taught to extend rules to new cases, starting with simple examples. For example, once students know how to add a pair of fractions with the same denominator, they can be asked to deduce for themselves how to add three fractions with the same denominator, how to subtract a pair of fractions with the same denominator, and how to proceed when addition and subtraction are combined.

As students learn to follow increasingly complex rules, and as they become adept at generalizing simple rules, they become motivated to remember and articulate why the rules for the various operations work as they do. Eventually, the teacher can return to concepts that were first presented as mechanical operations, adding layer after layer to students' understanding. The questions and exercises at the end of the fractions unit are to be introduced when students are ready. These exercises illustrate how to teach, in simple steps, concepts such as proportion and fractional equivalence. The teaching methods outlined above can easily be adapted to material that is normally considered beyond the reach of the majority of students. (Some educators believe that students should not be taught how to perform operations before they fully understand the concepts underlying the operations. I discuss this view in the Introduction to Part 2.)

A typical problem given to a Grade 6 enriched student runs as follows: "You have six blocks numbered one to six. You must build two towers, three blocks high, so that in each tower a block with a lower number never appears above a block with a higher number. How many solutions does this problem have?" If you give this problem to weaker students, they will likely have no idea how to begin. Even when they find an arrangement that satisfies the rule, they will not know how to determine whether they have found all valid arrangements.

Most teachers would conclude that the student was simply not mathematically minded, and that nothing could be done to change this fact. But a little reflection shows that the problem's solution requires only one skill, a skill that every working mathematician relies on to explore new mathematical terrain: the student must know only how to search systematically through a set of possible solutions, listing the ones that are valid. This skill can easily be taught. You might, for instance, give students three blocks numbered one to three and ask them to build a tower of two blocks satisfying the rule. You could even prepare them by asking, "Could the block with three on it appear on the bottom?" (thus introducing the idea of a necessary condition for the solution of a problem). As students try different arrangements, you might teach them to list the solutions systematically, by first placing the block with one on the bottom, then the block with two. After they have solved the problem with three blocks you might ask them to find all arrangements of four blocks in a tower of three. In this way students are led to solve more complex instances of the problem on their own. The units in Part 2 of this book introduce, step-by-step, basic conceptual skills that underlie all mathematical work.

CHAPTER 4

The Failure of Failure

IN A TYPICAL ELEMENTARY CLASS, EVEN AMONG CHILDREN WHO are only eight years old, an enormous difference exists between the weakest and the strongest students. The most knowledgeable will be able to recite their multiplication tables to 12, while the most delayed have trouble counting by twos. The fastest will finish a page of work before the slowest have found their pencils. And the most eager will wave their hands to answer a question while the most distracted stare vacantly into space.

This gap in knowledge, ability, and motivation — which is already pronounced in Grade 3 and which grows steadily until, by Grade 9, students must be separated into streams — appears to make it impossible to teach mathematics in the classroom. A teacher working with the texts and resources now available for elementary students can expect at most one-third of their class to complete tests and assignments independently without making errors. The other two-thirds will not be able to read, write, add, multiply, reason, or concentrate well enough to carry out their work with a high degree of success.

Based on my work with the Grade 3 class described in Chapter 2, and on similar experiments conducted in five other classes ranging from Grade 3 to Grade 5, I am absolutely certain the gap I have described is an artefact of our system of education — an illusion that can be dispelled more quickly and with fewer resources than even the most optimistic educator might expect. In an elementary class, the gap can be eliminated, or closed to a point where it doesn't affect the quality of the mathematics program, simply by using several volunteers over several months.

JUMP was not initially designed for the classroom. I decided to adapt it for that setting only after several teachers who were impressed with the results of the program invited me to test the method with their students. Though the material I had developed for the manual was intended for students in Grade 5 and above, I tried the fractions unit with a Grade 3 class. If it worked there, I reasoned, no teacher in Grade 5 could say their students were too young or too delayed to do the work.

During my first lesson with the Grade 3 students, I began to wonder if I had been too ambitious in my choice of grade level. I had previously tutored students who were 10 or older, in groups of two or three: now I was faced with 25 eight-year-olds, in an inner-city school where many spoke English as a second language. Most of the children in the class didn't know their times tables, nor could they add or subtract readily in their heads. Several had been diagnosed as slow learners. Others clearly had trouble concentrating in a room full of children.

By the second week of lessons, the majority of the students, including one boy who had never answered out loud in class before, began to wave their hands whenever I asked a question. Sometimes a student who I thought was slower would finish the work ahead of one who was faster. Students who at first had needed constant encouragement to complete an assignment began to ask for extra work.

In the third week, the class asked if I could stay longer so they could do more math. Occasionally, I would have to stop the lesson so everyone could come to the board, one at a time, to show off their mastery of an operation. Even the weakest students were offended if they weren't given a bonus question of greater difficulty than their regular work.

By the fourth week, it was hard to predict who would finish a worksheet first. Some students were still more likely to do so than others, but the extra time needed by the slowest students was usually negligible.

By the fifth week, the students had all scored over 90% on a Grade 6–7 fractions test. They went on to complete a unit on multiplication and division one or two years beyond their grade level, and a unit on solving word problems using logic and systematic search. None of the students has needed extra tutorials to keep up with the class.

Public-school teachers in five other classes, including one special-education class, have duplicated these results. In each of these classes a JUMP teacher (Maggie Licata, Katie Baldwin, or I) taught one demonstration lesson per week with several tutors assisting. The regular teachers, working from the JUMP manual and worksheets I had prepared, taught the rest of the lessons. In most of the classes the teacher was assisted twice a week by one or two JUMP tutors, and several students received occasional tutoring at recess. All of the teachers took more than five weeks to complete the fractions unit (the average time was about seven weeks); I believe this was because they had only just learned the method. In every class the students completed the fraction test with a final mark of A. Most scored over 90%.

In light of these results, there seems to be no excuse for the present state of mathematical education in our schools. Teachers can be trained in the JUMP method in several weeks, and high-school co-op students, university students, parents, and people with flexible work schedules can be recruited to assist in classrooms during the day. As elementary classes are usually 40 minutes long, a person who volunteers for two hours can work in two or three classes. At JUMP we have found that 20 volunteers are sufficient to establish an effective tutoring program in mathematics for Grades 3 through 6 in a mid-sized school.

I don't mean, by advocating that schools recruit volunteers, to suggest that governments should be allowed to neglect their responsibilities; one full-time professional tutor in a school could replace two dozen volunteers. It will take a great deal of public pressure in these conservative times, however, to persuade politicians to provide money for tutors. I hope the results of JUMP will inspire parents and concerned citizens to hold governments — as well as publishers, school boards, and educators — accountable. No program in mathematics should be implemented in our schools before it is tested in classes of 25 to 30 students. If a teacher cannot be trained in several weeks to follow the program, and if a child cannot be expected, with minimal tutorial assistance, to complete assignments and tests with a high degree of success, then the program should not be allowed in the schools.

There are several principles on which any program that seeks to meet these standards must be founded. These principles, which I outline directly below, are not difficult to understand or implement. But I believe they have never been articulated or followed rigorously in our schools, if only because they would never have occurred to someone who has accepted the myth that mathematical ability is innate.

Any person who is committed to educating all children, not just the few who are initially more advanced than their peers, must begin by acknowledging that the gap I have described, though easy to close, exists among students in every school and at every grade level. Without acknowledging this, no amount of effort spent improving textbooks, training teachers, or developing sophisticated manipulatives and teaching aids will ever help the majority of students.

Before I began teaching the Grade 3 class, I prepared a series of worksheets of graduated difficulty. For most of the operations and concepts in the fractions unit, I made three worksheets labelled A, B, and C. On the A sheets, the denominators of the fractions were divisible by two, three, or five; on the B sheets by four and six; and on the C sheets by seven, eight, and nine. Some questions on the B or C sheets required several more steps to complete than those on the A sheets.

I made sure, before I introduced the worksheets, that every child in the class could count on their fingers (on one hand only) by twos, threes, and fives. Then I showed the class how to multiply by counting. To find the product of two and five, you count by fives until you have raised two fingers — the number you say when you raise your last finger is the answer. When I was certain everyone could multiply, either on their fingers or by memory, I introduced the worksheets. With each new concept or operation, I let the faster students work ahead on the B and C sheets while I helped the slower students on the A sheets. I would never move ahead until every child in the class had completed the A sheet for a particular concept. The weaker students were always allowed enough time to master a concept or operation completely, while the stronger students, who were given extra work, were never bored. After a month, as the weakest students began to catch up and work more efficiently, I needed fewer extra sheets. Several questions written on the board were usually enough to keep students who had finished their work ahead of the others busy.

I used graduated worksheets to teach the weaker and less knowledgeable students in the class exactly the same concepts and operations as their peers, albeit using lower times tables. When I tested the class, I used fractions that had appeared on the A sheets, so the weaker students could do as well as everyone else. After they had scored higher than 90% on their tests, these students were eager to learn new tables. On the A sheets for the next unit, I included questions that required multiplication by fours and sixes: a teacher could continue in this way until their students had memorized all of their tables.

I soon learned, in my lessons with the Grade 3 class, not to underestimate how hard it is to convey information efficiently to a group of 25 children. Even in private tutorials, a task as simple as copying a symbol correctly can be hard for a child. In the classroom, where there are countless distractions, and where the teacher cannot pay attention to every student, such tasks are even more difficult.

A teacher who wishes to ensure that all of their students will succeed in mathematics must start by introducing information in steps that are virtually impossible to misinterpret. When I taught the Grade 3 class to add fractions with denominators that were different, I spent the first five minutes simply making sure everyone was able to place the times signs in the correct positions. I was able to cover more steps at once as the children became more confident and attentive, and more adept at copying questions quickly from the board and carrying out complex operations. But if I saw that any students were struggling, I would only ask them to perform a step as simple as counting on their fingers or copying a symbol. (It is possible to teach all elementary mathematics in this way, as the units in Part 2 of this book illustrate.) By introducing new information in mechanical steps, and by allowing enough repetition, I was able to cover far more material than if I had omitted steps.

Just as a footnote: children enjoy discovering mathematical ideas for themselves, through experiments and open-ended activities. But this method of teaching should not, I believe, be used extensively in a large classroom until a teacher is certain the entire class has developed the numerical and logical skills, as well as the confidence and motivation, to do this kind of work. The enriched units in the JUMP manual are based on this style of teaching, but these units are introduced only after students have completed a number of more basic units in which they are guided in small steps.

I am quite willing to believe that a mathematics program very different from the one I advocate, even one based entirely on exploration and open-ended activities, might be superior to JUMP. But any such approach should be formulated in rigorous detail by its proponents and tested exhaustively in large classrooms with teachers who are not confident about math. If it doesn't work for every student in a class, it shouldn't be used.

The method of teaching in steps is efficient, in part because it avoids a phenomenon that might well be called "interference." When a teacher introduces several pieces of information at the same time, students will often, in trying to comprehend the final item, lose all memory and understanding of the material that came before (even though they may have appeared to understand this material completely as it was being explained). With weaker students, it is always more efficient to introduce one piece of information at a time. When I teach rounding, for example, I start with numbers where the student has to round down, first to the nearest tens, then to the nearest hundreds, and so on. Then I repeat this process with numbers that round up. If I mix numbers that round up with ones that round down, as well as numbers that must be rounded to different place values, I will progress much more slowly than if I separate the various kinds of questions (this is particularly true in the classroom, where there are so many distractions).

This step-by-step method can serve to educate teachers as well as students, as it allows teachers to relearn math properly through teaching it. A Grade 4 teacher recently told me she had never understood the concept of probability, even though she had been required to teach it for a number of years. On two occasions, she had seen it demonstrated in her classroom, with sophisticated manipulatives, but she hadn't been able to reproduce the lesson. After reading the JUMP manual, she was able to teach the subject confidently for the first time.

In fact, many elementary teachers will admit to being as terrified of mathematics as their students. We would see a vast improvement in the teaching of mathematics in our schools if texts and teaching materials were written in meticulous, well-formulated steps, where teachers were shown exactly how to proceed at every point.

In my lessons, I tried to give the third graders a perspective on mathematics (and on learning in general) different from the one they had been taught since kindergarten. The atmosphere I set out to create in the class (with the help of the teacher and the tutors) was as essential to the success of the experiment as the step-by-step method I've been describing.

In my first lesson, I told my students that many things in mathematics take practice and getting used to, so they should never assume they were stupid when they found something hard. I told them that as a child I had thought I was stupid myself, but that I eventually discovered new things in mathematics on my own. I assured them they were all smart enough to do well in the subject. If something I presented was unclear, it would be my fault for failing to explain it, not theirs for failing to understand. I asked them to tell me whenever they were lost, so I could make sure they received help.

To anyone who has not observed the results of JUMP in the classroom, these assurances might well seem misguided or unrealistic. A teacher accustomed to watching students struggle with math will almost certainly balk at telling an entire class they can excel in the subject. A former teacher who volunteered for JUMP initially refused to tell her JUMP students they were smart, because, as she put it, "Not all children can be smart." And several teachers who tested JUMP with their classes only began to encourage their students sufficiently after children they thought were unteachable began to flourish.

When I agreed to test JUMP in classrooms, I hadn't foreseen how quickly an entire class would respond to a simple promise that they would all do well. In the classes where JUMP was tested, it took one or two weeks for the most difficult students to participate enthusiastically in lessons. In hindsight, I might have anticipated such results. Older children are often too cynical to care about doing well at school, or too bored to believe that a subject like math could ever be interesting. The ones who fall behind develop sophisticated defences to cope with failure. But younger children, who haven't been robbed of their natural curiosity or of their desire to be doted on by adults, will absorb knowledge without effort if they believe they can do it.

A program that allows children the luxury of success also allows teachers the luxury of giving them praise. This approach may take some getting used to for some teachers, especially those who have learned to rely on more traditional means (such as guilt, fear, or anger) to motivate their students, or who are afraid to encourage false hopes. Some styles of teaching are hard to abandon, even for teachers committed to the ideals of JUMP. Several months ago I watched a teacher who was learning the JUMP method help a boy with an operation from the fractions unit. She had followed the steps in the manual closely, but every time her student made a mistake she would say, with a hint of exasperation in her voice, "Why did you do it that way?" as though the boy had chosen to do the operation incorrectly. It took only a few minutes for the student to become flustered. The teacher pulled me aside and said, "I don't understand why he doesn't get it; he's normally one of the fastest students." When I told the boy that he had made a very good effort, but he had simply neglected to understand one thing, he was able to perform the operation right away.

I am not saying a teacher must always adopt the same tone with students: I can be quite firm with students who aren't working or paying attention. As well, I sometimes pretend to believe students can't do something so they can prove me wrong. But ultimately the students always know that I am impressed with them.

When a class works as a body, the students are carried forward by a common excitement. To maintain a sense of momentum in the class, it helps to have an assistant in the room several times a week, especially when new concepts are introduced. It also helps, in the first few months of the program, to have several extra tutors on hand once a week, so that students who are extremely delayed, unmotivated, or inattentive can be given lessons individually, or in small groups. Three or four students in each class needed this extra help in the classes where JUMP was tested. With most of these students, the extra tutoring was only required for a few months: a girl in Grade 4 who had received no formal schooling and who could barely count when she started the fractions unit needed only two months of weekly 40-minute tutorials to become one of the top students in the class (she received 98% on her fractions test). A boy in the same class who couldn't concentrate well enough to take part in lessons or complete assignments now always waves his hand to answer questions.

A teacher who kept their weakest students in at recess or after school several times a week might be able to match the results of a program with tutors. I think it is unreasonable, however, to expect this extra work of teachers: from what I have observed, they are already overtaxed managing 25 to 30 students. If we cared about educating children, our teachers would be given more support in the classroom, particularly in the early grades.

I was glad, in my first lessons with the Grade 3 students, to have an assistant in the class to help with those who were delayed or unmotivated. Whenever I demonstrated a step, the teacher and I would walk from desk to desk, making sure these students could repeat the step. After several weeks, however, I found I needed an assistant for an entirely different reason. As all of the students were beginning to complete their work without errors, the ones who had needed help would race to finish their assignments so they could be given a mark. They were thrilled to be able to call an adult to their desks to write, "Wow," or "Excellent," or "Perfect" in their books. For many, it was the first time they had received such praise at school.

I will never forget the moment I saw the aspect of the educational system that most impedes learning. I was standing in a room full of excited children who were all boisterously calling for the tutors to come and mark their work. It struck me how different the scene would be if, instead of As and A-pluses, the tutors were writing Cs and Ds in half of the children's books. With infants, the capacity to absorb knowledge cannot be separated from the capacity to be adored. It seems likely, from the way the most difficult students flourish in JUMP, that this is still true of children who are 10 and 11 years old. Otherwise, why would children with such different needs and impairments, ranging from severe psychological and behavioural problems to dyslexia and attention deficits, respond so quickly and in such a similar manner to the prospect of learning mathematics?

If children need to feel admired in order to learn, it follows that a system of education that measures or rewards their progress by assigning them a rank will never be as productive as one in which they are all expected to meet (roughly) the same standard. When only a fraction of a class receives a mark that is considered good, the majority will inevitably convince themselves that the subjects they did poorly in are difficult or boring.

I'm not advocating that children be given inflated marks to make them feel good. The marks the Grade 3 students received on my fractions test were an accurate measure of their ability to manipulate fractions. Indeed, the results of JUMP show that schools could set a standard, much higher than the one they have adopted, that every child could be expected to meet.

In a court of law, only adults are held accountable for their actions. In schools, however, children who are lazy or uncooperative are often treated as if they have made a free and informed decision to receive a grade of D or F. If children are more like infants than adults, then adults, not children, should be held responsible when a child fails. Adults should provide encouragement and rewards, as well as the attention that drives healthy children to learn from the day they are born.

Tests would not be used as threats or as measures of rank in a system that assumed education was the right of every child; they would serve as a way to guarantee that a child was not being neglected and as certificates and rewards for a child's work. In the Grade 3 class I taught, children who were absent for the fraction test nagged me until I allowed them to write it: for them, the test was a chance to show what they had learned.

Schools cannot be improved simply by compelling students to write standardized tests, as many politicians seem to believe. Tests accomplish nothing if teachers aren't trained or provided with the means to prepare students to do well on those tests.

After seeing how children flourish with even a modest amount of attention, I have come to believe that when a child fails a test it should be regarded as a failure of our system of education. And that when millions of children, year after year, fail tests they could easily pass, it should be regarded as the failure of an entire society to care for its young.

The costs of neglecting so many children are mounting, especially in neighbourhoods where parents cannot afford to hire tutors for their children. Hundreds of children would have fallen behind if not for the volunteers of JUMP alone. For want of classroom assistants, effective texts, and trained teachers, millions of other children will become convinced that they are bad at math before they graduate from school. It is disheartening to think of the potential wasted in our schools, and of the myths that will excuse this waste, until the day children are granted their right to be educated, and there is no mark assigned for failure.

CHAPTER 5

Breaking the Cycle of Ignorance

ONE OF THE JUMP TUTORS, HILARY, A SUCCESSFUL ACTOR, was extremely nervous before her first lesson. She had dropped math in Grade 10 and was having second thoughts about teaching a subject that had always terrified her. When her student arrived, he was accompanied by his mother, who handed Hilary a stack of psychological assessments. The child apparently had an attention-deficit disorder as well as another disorder that prevented him from taking notes or writing. During his lesson, he occasionally appeared to fall asleep, his eyes rolling back in their sockets.

Hilary emerged at the end of the lesson looking rather shaken. I told her I would find her an easier student. But she said she was actually more afraid of the math. After six months, she covered all of the existing JUMP material with the boy, and I had to design new units specifically for her. When I called her with several weeks of work, it took her only 10 minutes to learn it over the phone.

One way to lose one's fear of mathematics is to teach it. Several JUMP tutors who dropped math in high school are now among our best instructors. Tutors who were once afraid of mathematics can empathize with their students. They are careful not to make a child feel stupid, or to skip steps in explaining concepts. As well, they often bring special skills from their own line of work: actors like Hilary, for instance, are good at conveying their sense of excitement to their students.

One of the goals of JUMP is to give people who are not mathematicians or educators the opportunity to relearn mathematics (or learn mathematics properly for the first time) by explaining it to children. Because our tutors aren't required to have a background in math, we have found it easy to recruit dedicated volunteers from all walks of life. Among the 200 volunteers currently working for JUMP, 5% at most are mathematicians, scientists, or teachers. The rest are high-school students, university students, actors, writers, artists, business people, tradespeople, and retired professionals. This year, our oldest students will volunteer as JUMP tutors in their old elementary schools. We plan to train our students to be tutors when they reach Grade 10.

Since it was established in my apartment four years ago, JUMP has tripled in size each year, growing from 8 tutors and 15 students to 200 volunteers and 1,500 students. In growing so quickly, we have relied on experienced tutors and staff to train and oversee new tutors. We have been able to maintain the quality of the program, in spite of its rapid growth, because the tutors all work from the same manual (in which the steps are laid out in a way anyone could follow), and because their students are all expected to pass the same tests (with a mark of 80% or higher). Three years from now, under our present business plan, we hope to provide tutors for 7,000 children in 40 schools.

Some educators who are otherwise supportive of JUMP are concerned that a charity that relies on the work of volunteers is beginning to fulfill a function that should be the responsibility of the public school system. I share this concern, but I believe organizations like JUMP will be obliged play a role in public education for some time. Though I look forward to a day when JUMP becomes obsolete, I am certain our society will never invest in tutors for children, or in proper support and training for teachers, until the benefits of having a genuinely educated population are demonstrated on a large scale. A poorly educated population, unfortunately, will never see the point in electing a government committed to producing a well-educated population.

Whenever we have needed some service or resource at JUMP, whether it was the advice of a lawyer or accountant, a donation of books, or extra tutoring for a needy child, someone has phoned offering to help. There seems to be a growing reservoir of goodwill in our society, waiting for an outlet. And yet, as environmental, economic, and social crises erupt on a scale that was previously unimaginable, we find ourselves incapable of taking rational, collective action to avert these crises. There may never have been a greater gap between our global ideals and the way we conduct our daily lives.

A simple example illustrates this point. Every year in our cities there are ever-more-frequent smog warnings, and more reports of respiratory problems brought on by air pollution. But how many parents of children suffering from such problems would make fuel efficiency or low emissions a priority in buying a car? How many would think twice about driving their children across the city to purchase something they needed? The majority of the people who graduate from our schools are not even able to spot a contradiction in a commercial that promises a sense of freedom and self-determination to anyone daring enough to buy the most environmentally damaging vehicle available and drive it through a pristine wilderness.

The problem illustrated by this example is, I believe, even deeper than the political debates that consume so much of our attention. These debates have never called into question the assumption that children are born with vastly different mental abilities, or that the majority can never be expected to learn to think and reason clearly about mathematics or the natural world. This view of children, accepted by conservatives and socialists alike, may well be the chief cause of humanity's most persistent problems, including poverty, inequity, and the destruction of the environment.

Whether one places one's hopes for resolving our problems in governments or the private sector, it seems obvious that no economic system can be expected to distribute the products of our labour fairly or efficiently if only a fraction of the members of our society have the ability to weigh the costs and benefits of producing or buying various goods, or the ability to extrapolate or foresee how the effects of their purchases will add up. Before we can determine the best kind of economy to satisfy our material needs, we may have to raise a generation whose needs are less selfish and irrational than ours.

Recently in Ontario, the president of a major parents' organization told a reporter he approved of the newly introduced curriculum in mathematics because, in his words, "It will afford my son more opportunities to compete in the world." Sadly, the opportunity to "compete in the world" is the only reward a typical parent can promise children who wonder why they should study a subject they hate. For most parents, the necessity of vying for a job was the only reason they could see for studying math themselves. But while a facility with numbers will certainly help a person find employment, this is hardly the only thing that can be gained from an education in mathematics.

If schools were allowed to build walls around our national parks, and the majority of children were prevented from entering on the grounds that they lacked the ability to appreciate or understand what was inside, we might say something had been stolen from those children. And if the majority of children were convinced by their teachers that there was nothing beautiful or moving in the sight of a snow-capped mountain or a sky full of stars, we might be concerned that they had been stunted in their emotional or spiritual growth. But an equally beautiful part of nature has been made inaccessible to almost every child, and no one has noticed the loss.

Mathematicians often describe mathematics as a spiritual activity. This, of course, is surprising to most people. But mathematics, after all, is simply a different way of perceiving nature. It is a way of seeing symmetries and hidden connections that transcend the human imagination, a way of entering worlds so elegant and surprising they inspire a sense of awe. At JUMP we hope to encourage children to appreciate nature with all their faculties, allowing them to develop a deeper respect for the interconnectedness of all living and non-living things. At an early age they will be introduced, through games and enriched units, to the mathematics that underlies contemporary science — topology, group theory, graph theory, and chaos theory — as well as to new mathematics stemming from chemistry, biology, and computer science. Logic, argument analysis, and even the mathematics of the environment (how our actions add up) will be taught. Eventually we hope to develop lessons in philosophy and the arts.

There is no scarcity in the world of ideas; when someone understands an idea, its beauty is not consumed or used up. But everything in our present system of education seems designed to make real knowledge scarce, to keep the deepest ideas out of the hands of all but a few. If they are lucky, students graduating from high school will likely believe that they have one or two talents and that the majority of subjects offered at school are either uninteresting or beyond their grasp. In this sense our schools are quite efficient: 12 years is a relatively short time in which to close so many doors forever.

Though the developed countries of the world presently have the resources to feed and educate everyone on earth, more than half the world's children still live in abject poverty. In affluent countries, violence, overconsumption, and the destruction of the environment continue at the same pace. JUMP was founded in reaction to the institutionalized apathy and ignorance that underlie these problems. Children who grow up frustrated and insecure, meeting only a fraction of their potential, unable to reason clearly or weigh the consequences of their actions, and having witnessed few models of effective charity, will be exploited and misled with ease by corporations and politicians seeking gain. Until educated people devote themselves to breaking this cycle of ignorance, no amount of political action is likely to improve our condition.

The profound love parents feel for their children, the money and time they lavish on their families, have, to this day, been insufficient to change the world. Until we reach beyond our families to children in need, we will continue to neglect the needs of the children closest to us by passing on to them a world that is unfit to inherit.

PART 2

The JUMP Method

Approaches to Elementary Mathematics:
Selections from *The JUMP Teaching Manual*

Introduction

A HUNDRED YEARS AGO, RESEARCHERS IN LOGIC DISCOVERED that virtually all of the concepts used by working mathematicians could be reduced to one of two extremely basic operations, namely, the operation of counting or the operation of grouping objects into sets. Most people are able to perform both of these operations before they enter kindergarten. It is surprising, therefore, that schools have managed to make mathematics a mystery to so many students.

The following chapters contain excerpts from *The JUMP Teaching Manual*. The units selected for this book are only a small part of the JUMP program and do not cover the full elementary curriculum. They do, however, give a fairly complete picture of the method of teaching used in JUMP. The units are intended as models or templates: a teacher or parent can easily adapt the techniques introduced here to teach any topic in elementary mathematics.

The units in Chapters 6 and 7, which contain material on fractions and on multiplication and division, are among the most basic units in the JUMP manual. They demonstrate how a teacher can reduce mathematics to simple operations, such as counting and grouping objects into sets, that any student can perform. The unit in

Chapter 9 on ratios and percents shows how this approach can be extended to more advanced material. (The units from the manual in Chapters 6, 7, and 9 are not complete: they should be supplemented with conceptual exercises of the sort introduced at the end of Chapter 6.)

It is not the intention of the JUMP program to produce students who can only do mathematics by rote, or who experience mathematics as an endless series of mechanical drills. Even in the most basic units, students are expected to explain how operations work and generalize rules to deal with new cases by themselves. A student who has completed these units should have acquired the skills and the motivation to begin more independent work in mathematics. The units in Chapters 8, 10, and 11 show how a student can be led, through the systematic use of games, puzzles, and other activities, to solve problems and discover mathematical ideas on their own.

In Chapter 8, the notion of a coordinate system is introduced by means of a simple card trick. By figuring out how to perform the trick, students will learn (and likely remember) how the position of an object relative to an observer can be represented by a pair of numbers. And they will discover, by modifying the trick, several deep ideas about mathematics and space.

In Chapter 10, a method of teaching students to answer more open-ended mathematical questions is introduced. Mathematicians and scientists are often faced with problems that have more than one solution, or problems in which a solution can only be found by searching among many possibilities. In school, students are usually introduced to problems of this sort in a manner that is very unstructured. Problems are presented in stories or real-world situations in which different concepts have been mixed. Usually the particular skills required to solve the problem have not been isolated. Often the language of the problem is a barrier to children who have trouble reading English. In Chapter 10, all of the terms a student will need to answer a question are introduced in preparatory exercises. As well, students are shown how to solve more advanced problems by first working on "toy" models of a problem.

Chapter 11 introduces the notion of a finite state automaton, a simple model of a computer that can be played like a board game. By designing and writing a code for this model, a student will learn how a working computer can be represented by a string of letters. And by feeding data into their finite state automata, they will discover how a computer performs basic functions, such as identifying patterns in numbers and codes.

In teaching mathematics I often use simple diagrams or concrete materials. A finite state automaton can be "built" using a penny, a piece of paper, and a pencil. The notion of fractional equivalence can be taught using coloured blocks (Chapter 6), and objects in sets may be represented by lines inside boxes (Chapter 7). In abstract mathematics, the ability to draw a picture or create a model in which only the essential features of a problem are represented is an essential skill. Teachers may use more sophisticated manipulatives to supplement the units if they wish. With a delayed student, however, teachers should follow the mechanical procedures of the fractions unit very strictly. In classrooms where we have tested the JUMP method, students who had been struggling showed marked improvements in motivation and ability in a matter of weeks. They found it easier to work with concrete materials after they had finished the unit.

Students in Ontario must demonstrate a solid understanding of mathematical concepts to meet the requirements of the elementary curriculum: they must be capable of explaining how they found solutions to problems and of applying their knowledge in novel situations. Why, then, in the fractions unit of *The Jump Teaching Manual*, are operations introduced in entirely mechanical steps (and why at a level beyond current expectations for elementary students)? I have described already the enthusiasm that spreads contagiously through a class when students believe they are capable of learning material beyond their grade level. A teacher will find it hard to generate this kind of enthusiasm if they allow even a third of their class to feel they have no aptitude for mathematics. The fractions unit is designed specifically to help a teacher capture the attention of their weakest students and to build the basic mathematical skills those students need to progress to more advanced conceptual work. (See Chapters 3 and 6 for an account of these skills.)

None of the exercises in the first 15 sections of the fractions unit requires a mastery of English or of higher-order concepts. Students who speak English as a second language (a growing part of the population in many schools), students who are delayed in reading or writing, and students who have fallen behind academically are allowed the same chance to succeed as their peers. To do well on the Advanced Fractions Test (see page 113), students must simply perform the various operations introduced in the unit correctly. (The units that follow the fractions unit in the JUMP manual gradually introduce more conceptual work.)

Often the teachers who have seen their weakest students succeed on the fractions test are changed by the experience: they become more conscientious about breaking explanations into steps and are less likely to underestimate their students. The fractions unit is as much a test of a teacher's ability to teach the weakest students in their class as it is of a student's mastery of operations involving fractions.

Teachers who try the fractions unit but find they are leaving students behind should ask: Can all of my students multiply without hesitation by twos, threes, and fives (as taught in section F-1 of the unit)? Am I being careful to isolate the most basic steps in the operations? Am I teaching one step at a time and allowing enough repetition? Am I following the hints given in the unit for teaching weaker students? Am I expecting my students to learn or remember things that aren't relevant to the steps I'm trying to teach? Am I building momentum in my lessons by allowing all of my students to succeed? Am I giving sufficient encouragement? Am I spending extra time with my weaker students and giving them extra practice? Am I excited about my students' progress? Do I believe that all of my students (even those diagnosed with severe learning disabilities) can learn mathematics?

Some educators believe that teachers can actually arrest or delay the intellectual development of their students by teaching them how to perform an operation (such as adding fractions) before they have learned the concepts underlying the operation. However, while it is true that children who understand mathematics should ultimately be able to explain how they found a solution to a problem or why a rule works, it does not follow that a child who initially learns an operation by rote has no hope of learning the concept later. I learned fractions by rote and I think I can claim to understand fractions.

The idea that it is always harmful to teach rules before concepts is not supported by the actual practice of mathematics. John von Neumann, one of the great mathematicians of the 20th century, said that understanding mathematics is generally a matter of getting used to things. Mathematicians often approach difficult concepts by becoming familiar first with the rules and operations associated with the concepts. (In many branches of abstract mathematics, rules and concepts are hard to distinguish from each other.) To test a child's understanding of mathematics only by testing their grasp of concepts (while overlooking their mastery of rules and operations) is to neglect an important part of a child's education. Students who can add and subtract fractions without making errors already understand a good deal about fractions.

Mathematical discoveries are often based on ideas that are incomplete or partially false. Even in the mind of a mathematician, a concept will seldom arrive full-blown. A well-designed curriculum, therefore, will not penalize children academically or cause them to become discouraged if they fail to understand a concept immediately. As children mature, they acquire concepts naturally, through experience in the world. I have taught a number of adults to understand fractions in less than an hour. Even those who claimed to be hopeless in mathematics at school were shocked to see how quickly they could learn as adults.

In spite of the views I have expressed above, I believe that it is generally better to teach concepts before rules and that, whenever possible, children should be allowed to discover mathematical principles on their own. In schools where JUMP has raised the level of the students, mathematics is taught more conceptually each year. But in schools where children have been neglected, the benefits of starting with small steps far outweigh the disadvantages. All students are taken through the elementary curriculum at the same pace, with as much guidance as they need, until they have developed the confidence and skills they will require to explore more substantial mathematics.

CHAPTER 6

Fractions

MANY OF THE STUDENTS RECOMMENDED FOR JUMP DO NOT know any times tables when they start the program. It might seem pointless, therefore, to teach these students fractions right away. After all, they have a very poor sense of numbers and cannot be expected to find the lowest common denominator of a pair of fractions. I have found, however, that fractions are an ideal place to start. With fractions, complex operations can be reduced to steps any student can reproduce. In mastering these operations, even the most delayed students in JUMP have shown remarkable improvements in memory, concentration, and numerical and conceptual ability.

To teach this unit effectively you should bear in mind that its purpose is as much psychological as mathematical: the material is designed to train a student's attention and build confidence. Students who learn how to multiply and divide in the course of performing more difficult operations are motivated to remember their times tables. As well, a great deal of conceptual work is learned while performing the apparently mechanical procedures of this unit. Students learn to recognize patterns, select appropriate algorithms, and carry out complex sequences of operations. The goal of even the most mechanical exercise in the unit is to prepare children for more advanced conceptual mathematics.

Sections F-16 to F-20 contain conceptual exercises, which teach the notion of fractional equivalence. You may introduce these sections at any point in the unit, as long as your student knows how to divide (division is taught in F-5). In teaching a more delayed student, you might cover sections F-1 to F-15 and give your student the Advanced Fraction Test before you cover sections F-16 to F-20. After your student has done well on the fractions test, they will be more motivated to learn and remember the concepts underlying sections F-1 to F-15. (If you feel your student needs a break from fractions when they finish the fractions test, you might teach sections F-16 to F-20 after you have completed one or two other units.)

F-1: Counting

First check whether your student can count on one hand by twos, threes, and fives. If they can't, you will have to teach them. I've found the best way to do this is to draw a hand like this:

Have your student practise for a minute or two with the diagram, then without. When your student can count by twos, threes, and fives, teach them to multiply using their fingers, as follows:

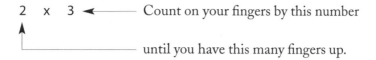

2 x 3 ◄————— Count on your fingers by this number

       └——————————— until you have this many fingers up.

The number you reach is the answer.

Give your student practice with questions like:

4 x 5 = ___   3 x 3 = ___   5 x 2 = ___

2 x 3 = ___   3 x 5 = ___   4 x 5 = ___

Point out that 2 x 3 means: add three, two times (that's what you are doing as you count up on your fingers). Don't belabour this point, though — you can explain it in more depth when your student is further into the units.

Your student should be able to count and multiply with ease by twos, threes, and fives on one hand before you teach the next section. As it is important to create a sense of momentum in your lessons (while still teaching by steps and allowing lots of repetition), you shouldn't expect a more delayed student to learn any table other than the fours (on one hand) as you progress through the rest of the unit. After your student has written the Fractions Test, you can introduce higher tables. (You can demand more of a more motivated or knowledge-able student: you might draw a new hand on their homework every few weeks and ask them to memorize it. You might also assign questions where they are required to use higher tables.)

F-2: Naming Fractions

Explain how to represent a fraction.

$\dfrac{3}{8}$ ← ——— **Step 1:** Count the number of shaded regions.

    ← ——— **Step 2:** Count the number of pieces the pie is cut into.

Remember, each step should be taught separately (allowing for repetition), unless your student is very quick.

Here are some questions your student can try:

What fraction of each figure is shaded?

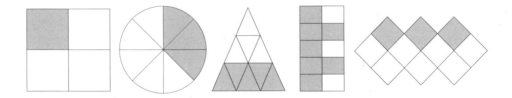

Make sure your student can name the *numerator* (top) and *denominator* (bottom). And that they know that the bigger the denominator, the more pieces the pie is cut into, and hence the smaller the piece size; that is, given two fractions, each with the number one in the numerator, the fraction with the larger denominator represents a smaller piece of the pie (because the pie is cut into more pieces). For instance, $\frac{1}{4}$ is smaller than $\frac{1}{3}$. (Draw this for your student.)

Teach your student how to draw $\frac{1}{2}$ and $\frac{1}{4}$ with circles.

Teach them how to draw $^1/_3$ as follows:

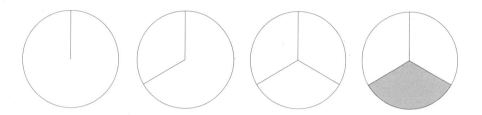

Ask your student how they would draw $^1/_2$ and $^1/_4$ in a square box. Make sure they know that in drawing a fraction, you have to make all the pieces the same size. For instance, this is *not* a good example of $^1/_4$:

Your student should be able to recognize when a shaded piece of pie is less than $^1/_2$ of a pie.

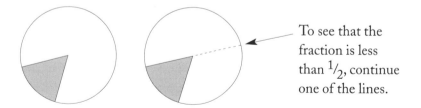

To see that the fraction is less than $^1/_2$, continue one of the lines.

F-3: Adding Two Fractions with the Same Denominator

Rule: Add the numerator and leave the denominator the same.

Example:

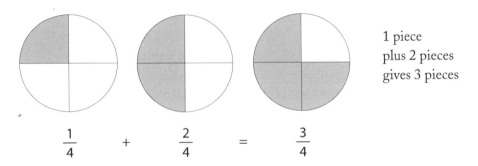

$$\frac{1}{4} \quad + \quad \frac{2}{4} \quad = \quad \frac{3}{4}$$

1 piece
plus 2 pieces
gives 3 pieces

Make sure your student knows why the denominator does not change: the pie is still cut into 4 pieces — you are still adding up $\frac{1}{4}$ size pieces.

Allow for lots of practice. Introduce one step at a time.

Whenever possible, you should allow the student to figure out how to extend a concept to a case they haven't seen. This is easy to do with the addition of fractions. Ask your student what they might do if:

• There were three fractions with the same denominator.

$$\frac{1}{7} \quad + \quad \frac{2}{7} \quad + \quad \frac{4}{7} \quad = \quad ?$$

(If your student guesses what to do in this case, point out that they are smart enough to figure out mathematical rules by themselves. It is essential that you make your student feel intelligent and capable right from the first lesson.)

- They had subtraction.

$$\frac{3}{4} - \frac{1}{4} = ?$$

Demonstrate this with a picture:

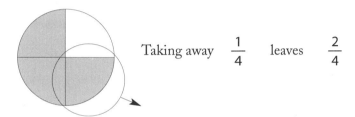

Taking away $\dfrac{1}{4}$ leaves $\dfrac{2}{4}$

- They had mixed addition and subtraction.

$$\frac{5}{7} + \frac{1}{7} - \frac{3}{7} = ?$$

Here are some sample questions you can use during this lesson (don't ask your student to reduce answers — this comes later, in section F-8):

(1) $\dfrac{1}{3} + \dfrac{1}{3}$ (2) $\dfrac{2}{7} + \dfrac{3}{7}$ (3) $\dfrac{2}{11} + \dfrac{10}{11}$

(4) $\dfrac{1}{20} + \dfrac{10}{20}$ (5) $\dfrac{2}{6} + \dfrac{3}{6}$ (6) $\dfrac{1}{15} + \dfrac{2}{15} + \dfrac{5}{15}$

(7) $\dfrac{1}{7} + \dfrac{2}{7} + \dfrac{3}{7}$ (8) $\dfrac{5}{7} + \dfrac{1}{7}$ (9) $\dfrac{4}{4} - \dfrac{1}{4}$

(10) $\dfrac{4}{8} - \dfrac{3}{8}$ (11) $\dfrac{2}{11} + \dfrac{5}{11} - \dfrac{3}{11}$ (12) $\dfrac{3}{20} + \dfrac{8}{20} - \dfrac{6}{20}$

F-4: Adding Fractions with Different Denominators

If the denominators are different, then you can't compare piece sizes — it's not clear how to add fractions with different denominators.

Example:

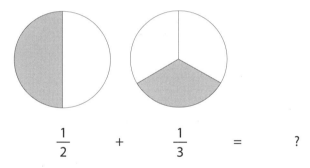

$$\dfrac{1}{2} \quad + \quad \dfrac{1}{3} \quad = \quad ?$$

Tell your student that after you have shown them how the operation works with pictures you will show them a much easier method they cannot fail to perform. (You should, however, return to this sort of pictorial explanation when your student fully masters the operation.)

Solution: Cut each of the two pieces in the first pie into three, and cut each of the three pieces in the second pie into two. This will give the same number of pieces in each because 2 x 3 = 3 x 2 = 6

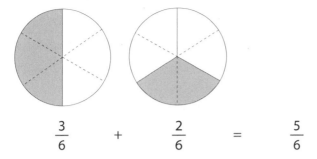

$$\frac{3}{6} \quad + \quad \frac{2}{6} \quad = \quad \frac{5}{6}$$

Draw the above picture and ask your student to write the new fractions corresponding to the way pies are now cut. Make sure they notice that $\frac{1}{2}$ is the same as $\frac{3}{6}$ of the pie, and that $\frac{1}{3}$ is the same as $\frac{2}{6}$ (and one out of three pieces is the same as two out of six). Once you have discussed this, your student can perform the addition. Here is the one thing the student should take away from this explanation: to produce pieces of the same size in both pies (which is necessary for adding fractions), one has to cut each pie into smaller pieces. (For more advanced students: the number of pieces you need to cut both pies into is equal to the lowest common multiple of the denominators — see section F-9.)

Tell your student you will now teach them a very easy way of changing the number of pieces the pie is cut into without having to draw the picture.

Step 1: Multiply each denominator by the other one. The numerator also has to be multiplied, because now you are getting more pieces:

$$\frac{3 \times 1}{3 \times 2} + \frac{1 \times 2}{3 \times 2}$$

Have your student practise this step before you go on. The student should just practise setting the right numbers in the right places. Remember you can make this step easier if necessary by having the student move one denominator at a time (see Chapter 3, pages 28–30).

Step 2: Perform the multiplication.

$$\frac{3 \times 1}{3 \times 2} + \frac{1 \times 2}{3 \times 2} = \frac{3}{6} + \frac{2}{6}$$

Practise step 1, then step 1 and step 2 together, before you go on.

Step 3: Perform the addition.

$$\frac{3}{6} + \frac{2}{6} = \frac{5}{6}$$

Now have the student practise all three steps.

Here are some sample questions you can use during this lesson:

(1) $\frac{1}{2} + \frac{1}{3}$ (2) $\frac{1}{3} + \frac{1}{5}$ (3) $\frac{1}{3} + \frac{1}{4}$

(4) $\frac{1}{2} + \frac{1}{5}$ (5) $\frac{2}{3} + \frac{1}{4}$ (6) $\frac{3}{5} + \frac{1}{2}$

(7) $\frac{3}{4} + \frac{2}{3}$ (8) $\frac{3}{5} + \frac{1}{4}$ (9) $\frac{2}{3} + \frac{4}{5}$

(10) $\frac{4}{5} + \frac{1}{2}$ (11) $\frac{2}{3} - \frac{1}{2}$ (12) $\frac{4}{5} - \frac{1}{3}$

For students who know higher times tables, gradually mix in higher denominators like 6 and 7 (make sure the smaller denominator does not divide the larger).

Note: Two numbers are relatively prime if their least-common multiple (the lowest number they both divide into evenly) is their product. For instance, 2 and 3 are relatively prime, but 4 and 6 are not (since the product of 4 and 6 is 24, while their least common multiple is 12). The method of adding fractions taught in this section is really efficient only for fractions whose denominators are relatively prime (as is the case for all of the examples on page 72). For other cases — for instance when one denominator divides into the other or when both denominators divide into a number that is smaller than their product — more efficient methods can be found in sections F-5 and F-9.

F-5: Changing One Denominator

Tell your student that sometimes you don't have to change both denominators when you add fractions. How can you tell when you can do less work?

Step 1: Check to see if the smaller denominator divides into the larger. Count up on your fingers by the smaller denominator and see if you hit the larger denominator — if you do, the number of fingers you have up is what you multiply the smaller denominator by:

$$\frac{1}{2} + \frac{1}{10} = \frac{5 \times 1}{5 \times 2} + \frac{1}{10}$$

Counting up by twos, you hit 10. You have 5 fingers up. This means 5 x 2 = 10

Multiply the smaller denominator by the number of fingers you have up.

Give lots of time for practice at this step before you move on.

Step 2: Perform the multiplication.

$$\frac{5 \times 1}{5 \times 2} + \frac{1}{10} = \frac{5}{10} + \frac{1}{10}$$

Step 3: Perform the addition.

$$\frac{5}{10} + \frac{1}{10} = \frac{6}{10}$$

Extra: Ask your student how they would do

$$\frac{1}{2} - \frac{1}{10} =$$

Here are some sample questions you can use during this lesson:

(1) $\frac{1}{2} + \frac{1}{10}$ (2) $\frac{3}{4} + \frac{1}{8}$ (3) $\frac{1}{5} + \frac{1}{10}$

(4) $\frac{1}{8} + \frac{1}{2}$ (5) $\frac{1}{3} + \frac{1}{6}$ (6) $\frac{1}{4} + \frac{1}{12}$

(7) $\frac{2}{3} + \frac{1}{15}$ (8) $\frac{1}{5} + \frac{1}{20}$ (9) $\frac{7}{25} + \frac{2}{5}$

(10) $\frac{1}{2} - \frac{1}{4}$ (11) $\frac{2}{3} - \frac{1}{9}$ (12) $\frac{7}{15} - \frac{1}{3}$

Note: If you think your student might have trouble with this section, you should start with the following exercise: tell your student that the number 2 "goes into" or "divides" the numbers they say when they are counting up by twos (2 divides 2, 4, 6, 8, 10, etc). Write several numbers between 2 and 10 in a column and ask your student to write "yes" beside the numbers that 2 goes into, and "no" beside the others. When your student has mastered this step, repeat the exercise with numbers between 3 and 15 (for counting by threes) and with numbers between 5 and 25 divisible by 5 (for counting by fives). Tell your student that when they are adding fractions, they should always check to see if the smaller denominator divides into the larger; when this is the case, they only have to change the smaller denominator.

F-6: Distinguishing Between the Three Methods Taught Thus Far

This is an important section. For many students, it may be the first time they are taught how to decide which of several algorithms they should use to perform an operation.

Tell your student always to follow these steps when given a pair of fractions to add:

Step 1: Check to see if the two denominators are the same. If yes, write "same." If no, go to step 2.

Step 2: Identify the smaller denominator. Count up by that number and see if you hit the larger denominator (i.e., see if the smaller divides or goes into the larger evenly). If yes, write "change one." If not, write "change both." (In other words, the student is identifying whether or not they will have to change one or both fractions before adding.)

Practise these steps on a variety of different pairs of fractions before going on.

Step 3: If the student has written "same," add the fractions using the procedure in F-3. If they have written "change both," follow the procedure in F-4, and if they have written "change one," follow the procedure in F-5.

Typical exercise:

(1) $\dfrac{1}{7} + \dfrac{2}{7}$ (2) $\dfrac{3}{5} + \dfrac{1}{15}$ (3) $\dfrac{3}{4} + \dfrac{1}{5}$

Give the student a number of pages on which you have mixed up the types of questions in sections F-3, F-4, and F-5. If you think your student might have trouble with this section, make sure they can recognize when one number divides into another (see the method described in the note of section F-5). Then try the following exercise:

Write a pair of fractions in which the denominator of the first fraction divides the denominator of the second fraction, and then write another pair of fractions in which the denominators are relatively prime. For, instance, you might write:

$$\frac{1}{2} + \frac{1}{6} \qquad \frac{1}{2} + \frac{1}{5}$$

Ask your student to find the pair where the smaller denominator divides into the larger and write "yes" beside it (and "no" beside the other pair). Have them repeat this step with other pairs, without adding the fractions, until they can tell when one denominator divides another. When your student masters this step, write down more than two pairs at a time and have them identify all the yeses and all the noes (without adding the fractions).

F-7: Adding Three Fractions

Let your student know that this is an enriched unit. Adding triple fractions is normally not covered until Grade 6 or 7.

Give questions where two smaller denominators go into the larger, for example:

$$\frac{1}{2} \;+\; \frac{1}{3} \;+\; \frac{1}{6}$$

$$\frac{3 \;\times\; 1}{3 \;\times\; 2} \;+\; \frac{1 \;\times\; 2}{3 \;\times\; 2} \;+\; \frac{1}{6}$$

$$\frac{3}{6} \;+\; \frac{2}{6} \;+\; \frac{1}{6} \;=\; \frac{6}{6}$$

Note: When you first teach this section, place the fractions with the two lowest denominators first. After your student has mastered this, you can change the order and ask them to identify which denominators have to be changed.

Here are some sample questions you can use during this lesson:

(1) $\dfrac{1}{2} \;+\; \dfrac{1}{3} \;+\; \dfrac{1}{6}$ (2) $\dfrac{2}{3} \;+\; \dfrac{1}{5} \;+\; \dfrac{1}{15}$

(3) $\dfrac{3}{4} \;+\; \dfrac{1}{2} \;+\; \dfrac{1}{8}$

F-8: Equivalent Fractions and Reducing Fractions

First check to see if your student knows how to divide by a single-digit number. If not, teach them as follows:

15 ÷ 3 = ?

Count up by the number that comes after the division sign until you reach the number in front of the sign; the number of fingers you have up is the answer; e.g., 3 divides 15 five times, because it takes five 3s to add up to 15. Give lots of practice. Then explain to your student that the same fraction can have different representations:

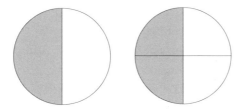

For instance, with $^1/_2$ of a pie and $^2/_4$ of a pie you get the same amount of pie.

Each fraction has a representation in the smallest possible whole numbers. Finding this representation is called reducing the fraction.

To check whether a fraction can be represented with smaller numbers, your student should check first whether the numerator divides into the denominator.

Step 1: $\dfrac{5}{15}$ Count up by the numerator to see if it divides into the denominator.

Step 2: If yes, divide both the numerator and the denominator of the fraction by the numerator:

$$\frac{5 \div 5}{15 \div 5} = \frac{1}{3}$$

Some students will need a good deal of practice with step 1. You might give your student a sheet of questions on which they simply have to count up by the numerator, checking to see if they say the denominator as they count.

Once your student has mastered the steps above, let them know that if the numerator of a fraction does not divide the denominator, they should still check to see if any smaller number divides both. If they find a number that goes into the numerator and the denominator, they should reduce the fraction as follows:

$$\frac{4 \div 2}{6 \div 2} = \frac{2}{3}$$

You might start by giving your student hints. You might say, for instance, "The numerator and denominator of this fraction divide by either 2 or by 3. Check which one works."

Here are some sample questions you can use during this lesson:

Division

(1) $25 \div 5$ (2) $16 \div 4$ (3) $8 \div 2$

(4) $12 \div 3$ (5) $15 \div 5$ (6) $6 \div 2$

(7) $10 \div 2$ (8) $20 \div 4$

Reducing fractions (easier)

(1) $\dfrac{5}{15}$ (2) $\dfrac{2}{8}$ (3) $\dfrac{2}{6}$ (4) $\dfrac{3}{6}$ (5) $\dfrac{3}{9}$ (6) $\dfrac{5}{25}$

(7) $\dfrac{5}{10}$ (8) $\dfrac{2}{10}$ (9) $\dfrac{3}{12}$ (10) $\dfrac{3}{15}$ (11) $\dfrac{5}{30}$ (12) $\dfrac{2}{12}$

Reducing fractions (harder)

(1) $\dfrac{4}{6}$ (2) $\dfrac{6}{8}$ (3) $\dfrac{8}{10}$ (4) $\dfrac{8}{12}$ (5) $\dfrac{6}{9}$ (6) $\dfrac{9}{15}$

(7) $\dfrac{9}{12}$ (8) $\dfrac{5}{10}$ (9) $\dfrac{10}{15}$ (10) $\dfrac{20}{25}$ (11) $\dfrac{15}{20}$ (12) $\dfrac{20}{30}$

Note: If your student has just learned to multiply, ask them only to reduce fractions where the numerator and denominator divide by 2, 3, or 5. You should give them the same questions repeatedly for homework as it may take them some time to get used to reducing.

F-9: Finding the Lowest Common Denominator

This section should only be taught to second-year JUMP students or to very advanced first years.

The lowest common multiple (LCM) of two numbers is the lowest number that both divide into evenly. For instance, the lowest common multiple of 4 and 6 is 12. Notice that the lowest common multiple of 4 and 6 *is lower than* their product (4 x 6 = 24). But with other numbers, say 2 and 3, the lowest common multiple *is* the product. To find the lowest common multiple of a pair of numbers, simply count up by the larger number and keep checking whether the smaller divides into the result.

Example: 4 and 6
Count up by sixes.
6: 4 does not go into 6. Keep counting up.
12: 4 goes into 12.
Therefore, LCM = 12

Example: 2 and 3
Count up by threes.
3: 2 does not go into 3. Keep counting up.
6: 2 goes into 6.
Therefore, LCM = 6

Example: 2 and 10
Count up by tens
10: 2 goes into 10.
Therefore, LCM = 10

By counting up, have your student find the LCM of the following pairs. Also have them say whether the LCM is equal to the product or less than the product.

(1)   3 and 5   (2)   2 and 8   (3)   4 and 6

(4)   4 and 10   (5)   5 and 10   (6)   6 and 9

(7)   2 and 10   (8)   5 and 4   (9)   3 and 4

(10)   6 and 8   (11)   8 and 10   (12)   2 and 7

The method of adding fractions that we taught in sections F-4 to F-6 doesn't always yield a final denominator that is the LCM of the two denominators; by our method the student would add $^1/_4$ and $^1/_6$ by changing both fractions as follows:

$$\frac{1}{4} + \frac{1}{6} \rightarrow \frac{6 \times 1}{6 \times 4} + \frac{1 \times 4}{6 \times 4} \rightarrow \frac{6}{24} + \frac{4}{24} \rightarrow \frac{10}{24}$$

$\dfrac{10}{24}$ can be reduced (see Section F-8) to $\dfrac{5}{12}$

If the student thinks that the LCM of a pair of denominators may be lower than the product, then (to avoid having to reduce the answer) they should proceed as follows:

To find the LCM, count up by the larger denominator (in this case 6) until you reach a number that the smaller denominator divides into. Counting by sixes you get 12, and you can stop counting there because 4 divides into 12, so the student can use 12 as the denominator:

$$\frac{1}{4} + \frac{1}{6} \rightarrow \frac{3 \times 1}{3 \times 4} + \frac{1 \times 2}{6 \times 2} \rightarrow \frac{3}{12} + \frac{2}{12} \rightarrow \frac{5}{12}$$

Make sure your student knows the LCM is also called the lowest common denominator.

Your student should try these questions:

(1) $\dfrac{1}{6} + \dfrac{3}{8}$ (2) $\dfrac{1}{6} + \dfrac{1}{10}$ (3) $\dfrac{3}{8} + \dfrac{5}{12}$

This method will also work for triple fractions.

$$\frac{1}{5} + \frac{1}{6} + \frac{1}{10}$$

Tell the student to count up by the largest denominator, and at each stage to check whether the smaller denominators divide the number they have reached. For instance: two 10s are 20, but 6 does not divide 20, so the student should keep counting by tens. Three 10s are 30, and 5 and 6 both divide 30, so the student should use 30 as the denominator.

Here are some sample (Grade 8 level) questions you can use during this lesson:

(1) $\frac{1}{4} + \frac{1}{3} + \frac{1}{6}$ (2) $\frac{1}{4} + \frac{1}{6} + \frac{1}{8}$

(3) $\frac{3}{5} + \frac{1}{6} + \frac{7}{10}$ (4) $\frac{1}{3} + \frac{5}{6} + \frac{1}{9}$

(5) $\frac{1}{8} + \frac{3}{6} + \frac{1}{12}$ (6) $\frac{1}{12} + \frac{1}{9} + \frac{1}{4}$

F-10: Mixed Fractions and Improper Fractions

If the numerator of a fraction is bigger than the denominator, the fraction is called an improper fraction. Any improper fraction can also be written as a mixed fraction, that is, as a combination of a whole number and a fraction. For instance:

$$\frac{3}{2} = 1\frac{1}{2}$$

You can explain these two ways of writing a fraction with a picture.

$\dfrac{3}{2}$ or $1\dfrac{1}{2}$

Three half-size pieces of a pie are the same as one whole pie, plus an extra half.

How to write a fraction as an improper fraction:

Example:

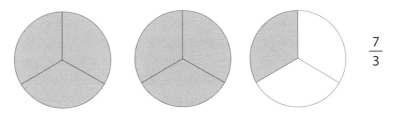

$\dfrac{7}{3}$

Step 1: How many pieces are shaded? Answer: 7. Put this number in the numerator.

Step 2: How many pieces is each pie cut into? Answer: 3. Put this number in the denominator. (Even though you have more than one pie, the piece size doesn't change — you still have third-size pieces in each pie — 7 all together.)

How to write a fraction as a mixed fraction:

Example:

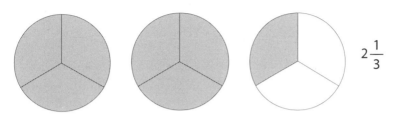

$2\dfrac{1}{3}$

Step 1: How many whole pies are there? Answer: 2. Write this down as a whole number.

Step 2: Write down what fraction of a pie you have in the last pie.

Give your student lots of practice in the two ways of writing a fraction. Here are some examples you might use:

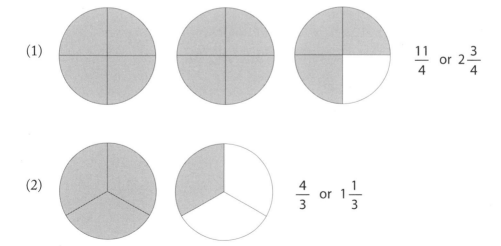

(1) $\dfrac{11}{4}$ or $2\dfrac{3}{4}$

(2) $\dfrac{4}{3}$ or $1\dfrac{1}{3}$

(3) 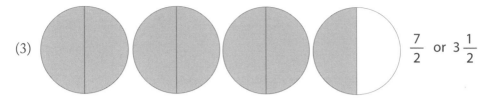 $\dfrac{7}{2}$ or $3\dfrac{1}{2}$

Your student should be able to draw simple mixed fractions like

$$1\frac{1}{2} \quad 2\frac{1}{2} \quad 1\frac{1}{3} \quad 2\frac{1}{3} \quad 1\frac{1}{4} \quad 1\frac{3}{4}$$

Your student should also be able to decide, in simple cases, which of two mixed fractions is larger. For instance,

$$2\frac{1}{2} \text{ or } 3\frac{1}{2} \quad 1\frac{1}{4} \text{ or } 2\frac{5}{6} \quad 1\frac{1}{3} \text{ or } 1\frac{1}{4}$$

Your student should be able to explain how they can tell when a fraction represents more than a whole pie: they should be able to say "when the top (or numerator) is larger than the bottom (or denominator) you have more than one pie."

As a test, write out several fractions and ask your student to identify the fractions that represent more than one whole pie. For instance,

$$(1)\ \frac{5}{6} \qquad (2)\ \frac{7}{4} \qquad (3)\ \frac{2}{3} \qquad (4)\ \frac{12}{5}$$

F-11: Converting Mixed Fractions into Improper Fractions

Step 2: $6 + 1 = 7$

Example: $2\dfrac{1}{3} = \dfrac{7}{3}$ ◄——— **Step 3**

Step 1: x

Step 1: Multiply the whole number by the denominator, i.e., 2 x 3 = 6. (To explain this step, point out that in two whole pies [each cut into three pieces], there are six pieces.)

Step 2: Add the number you got in the last step to the numerator. Put the sum in the numerator of your improper fraction. (To explain this step, point out that in the one-third pie you have one piece which has to be added to the six pieces in the two whole pies, giving seven pieces all together.)

Step 3: Write the denominator of the mixed fraction in the denominator of the improper fraction. (The two fractions have the same denominator because the piece size is still one-third.)

Here are some sample questions you can use during this lesson:

(1) $2\dfrac{1}{2}$ (2) $3\dfrac{1}{3}$ (3) $5\dfrac{1}{2}$ (4) $4\dfrac{1}{3}$ (5) $3\dfrac{2}{3}$ (6) $1\dfrac{1}{3}$

(7) $4\dfrac{1}{5}$ (8) $3\dfrac{4}{5}$ (9) $5\dfrac{2}{5}$ (10) $5\dfrac{2}{3}$ (11) $4\dfrac{3}{4}$ (12) $5\dfrac{1}{6}$

F-12: Converting Improper Fractions into Mixed Fractions

First, you may have to teach your student how to divide when the divisor doesn't go evenly into the number being divided.

Example: 2 | 9

Step 1: Count up on your fingers by the divisor (e.g., 2) until you reach a number just below the number being divided (9).

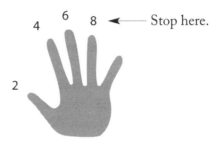

If the student has trouble knowing when they should stop counting up, practise this step with various examples:

    2 | 11   3 | 10   5 | 17

If your student is really struggling with this step, write the numbers from 1 to 10 and circle the numbers divisible by 2. This will help your student see when to stop counting. Repeat this with the numbers between 1 and 15 (for counting by threes) and 1 and 25 (for counting by fives).

Step 2: Write the number of fingers you have up on top of the division sign:

$$
\begin{array}{r}
4 \\
2 \overline{)9}
\end{array}
$$

Step 3: Write the number you reached on your fingers below the number being divided:

$$
\begin{array}{r}
4 \\
2 \overline{)9} \\
8
\end{array}
$$

Step 4: Subtract to find the remainder:

$$
\begin{array}{r}
4 \\
2 \overline{)9} \\
-8 \\
\hline
1
\end{array}
\qquad
\begin{array}{r}
4 \ \text{R}1 \\
2 \overline{)9} \\
-8 \\
\hline
1
\end{array}
$$

Explain that the answer on top means that 2 fits into 9 four times with 1 left over. You might draw a picture to illustrate this:

        | ◄———— remainder 1

How to convert an improper fraction into a mixed fraction:

Step 1: Rewrite the fraction as a division statement:

$$
\frac{9}{2} \qquad\qquad 2 \overline{)9}
$$

Have the student practise putting the right number in the right place.

Step 2: Do the long division. Your student should know how to do this from the previous section:

$$
\begin{array}{r}
4 \ \text{R} 1 \\
2 \ \overline{\big)\ 9} \\
-8 \\
\hline
1
\end{array}
$$

Step 3: Use the answer to the division problem to write the mixed fraction:

$$
\frac{9}{2} \ = \ 4\frac{1}{2}
\qquad\qquad
\begin{array}{r}
4 \ \text{R} 1 \\
2 \ \overline{\big)\ 9} \\
-8 \\
\hline
1
\end{array}
$$

After your student has learned to convert improper fractions to mixed fractions, teach them to estimate how many whole pies an improper fraction represents. For instance, $7/3$ is at least two whole pies because 3 divides into 7 two times (the remainder, 1, is the number of fractional pieces in the last pie plate).

Your student should be able to say, in simple cases, which of two improper fractions is larger. For instance, $7/2$ is larger than $11/5$ because in the first case you have three whole pies, and in the latter, two.

They should also be able to say when an improper fraction is bigger than a whole number. For instance, $7/3$ is bigger than 2.

Finally, your student should know that an improper fraction is always bigger than a proper fraction. You might write out several pairs and have them identify the larger; for instance, $5/6$ and $7/5$.

Here are some sample questions you can use during this lesson:

(1) $\dfrac{5}{2}$ (2) $\dfrac{7}{2}$ (3) $\dfrac{7}{3}$ (4) $\dfrac{9}{2}$ (5) $\dfrac{11}{3}$ (6) $\dfrac{9}{4}$

(7) $\dfrac{16}{5}$ (8) $\dfrac{12}{5}$ (9) $\dfrac{23}{5}$ (10) $\dfrac{17}{4}$ (11) $\dfrac{11}{2}$ (12) $\dfrac{17}{5}$

Note: Maggie Licata, the former executive director of JUMP, suggests a method for converting improper fractions to mixed fractions that I think is easier than the one I give above (her method also enables students to do the conversions in their heads). If you use the following method, you should still, at some point, teach your student how to do long division by the method above.

Change $\frac{9}{2}$ to a mixed fraction:

Step 1: Count by the denominator until you reach a number just below the number being divided. (This is just step 1, as outlined above.)

Step 2: Write the number of fingers you have raised (four fingers) as a whole number:
$$\frac{9}{2} = 4$$

Step 3: Write the denominator of the original fraction beside the whole number:
$$\frac{9}{2} = 4\,\overline{}_{2}$$

Step 4: Multiply the whole number by the denominator:
$$2 \ \times \ 4 \ = \ 8$$

Step 5: Subtract the result of step 4 from the numerator of the improper fraction:

$$9 \ - \ 8 \ = \ 1$$

Step 6: The answer from step 5 is the numerator of the mixed fraction:

$$\frac{9}{2} \ = \ 4\frac{1}{2}$$

If your student has trouble with step 5, teach them to subtract as follows:

$$17 \ - \ 15 \ = \ ?$$

Step 1: Say the second number ("15") with your fist closed.

Step 2: Raising one finger at a time, count until you reach the first number (the student raises one finger when they say "16" and another when they say "17"). The number of fingers you have up is the answer.

Give your student lots of practice at this. (Eventually you can give questions involving fairly large numbers such as $178 - 173$ to boost your student's confidence. Make sure the numbers you pick aren't too widely separated: for numbers that have a difference greater than 10, it is better to subtract by lining the numbers up in the traditional way.)

F-13: Adding Mixed Fractions

Converting fractions to improper fractions, then adding them.

Example: $1\frac{1}{2} \ + \ 2\frac{1}{4} \ = \ ?$

First, convert the fractions to improper fractions (see F-10):

$$1\frac{1}{2} + 2\frac{1}{4} = \frac{3}{2} + \frac{9}{4}$$

Now add the fractions (as taught in F-4 to F-6):

$$\frac{3}{2} + \frac{9}{4} = \frac{2 \times 3}{2 \times 2} + \frac{9}{4} = \frac{6}{4} + \frac{9}{4} = \frac{15}{4}$$

Here are some sample questions you can use during this lesson:

(1) $1\frac{1}{2} + 2\frac{1}{3}$ (2) $2\frac{1}{2} + 1\frac{1}{3}$ (3) $\frac{1}{2} + 1\frac{1}{5}$ (4) $2\frac{2}{3} + 3\frac{1}{4}$

(5) $2\frac{1}{2} + 1\frac{3}{4}$ (6) $3\frac{1}{2} + 5\frac{1}{4}$ (7) $\frac{2}{5} + 1\frac{1}{2}$ (8) $\frac{3}{4} + 2\frac{1}{5}$

Note: There is a method of adding fractions that is more efficient than the one taught above when the whole numbers or the denominators of the fractions are large. If your student finds fractions easy, you might teach them the following method. (Otherwise wait until your student has completed several other units of the manual.)

Example: $8\frac{1}{2} + 5\frac{1}{3} = ?$

Step 1: Make the denominators of the fractions the same (as you would if you were simply adding the fractions):

$$8\frac{1}{2} + 5\frac{1}{3} \longrightarrow 8\frac{1 \times 3}{2 \times 3} + 5\frac{1 \times 2}{2 \times 2} \longrightarrow 8\frac{3}{6} + 5\frac{2}{6}$$

Step 2: Add the whole numbers (8 and 5) and the fractions ($^3/_6$ and $^2/_6$) separately, but write your answer as a single mixed fraction:

$$8\frac{3}{6} + 5\frac{2}{6} \quad \longrightarrow \quad 13\frac{5}{6}$$

In some cases, the fractional part of the answer may be an improper fraction. For instance:

$$8\frac{1}{2} + 5\frac{2}{3} \longrightarrow 8\frac{1}{2} \begin{array}{c} \times \\ \times \end{array} \begin{array}{c} 3 \\ 3 \end{array} + 5\frac{2}{3} \begin{array}{c} \times \\ \times \end{array} \begin{array}{c} 2 \\ 2 \end{array} \longrightarrow 8\frac{3}{6} + 5\frac{4}{6} \longrightarrow 13\frac{7}{6}$$

In this case, your student should change their answer as follows:

Step 1: Rewrite your answer as the sum of a whole number and a fraction:

$$13\frac{7}{6} \quad = \quad 13 \quad + \quad \frac{7}{6}$$

Step 2: Rewrite the improper fraction as a mixed fraction (as taught in F-12):

$$13\frac{7}{6} \quad = \quad 13 \quad + \quad 1\frac{1}{6}$$

Step 3: Add:

$$13 \quad + \quad 1\frac{1}{6} \quad = \quad 14\frac{1}{6}$$

F-14: Comparing Fractions

First, teach your student the meaning of the "greater than" (>) and "less than" (<) signs. Tell them the arrow should always point from the larger number to the smaller number.

Example: 2 > 1 "Two is greater than one."
2 < 3 "Two is less than three."

Give the student practice filling in the sign with whole numbers.

Example: 7 ? 9 $\longrightarrow$ 7 < 9

Now, tell your student that to compare the size of two fractions they simply have to convert the fractions to the same denominator. The fraction with the larger numerator is the larger fraction.

Example:

$$\frac{2}{3} \; ? \; \frac{5}{6} \longrightarrow \frac{2 \times 2}{2 \times 2} \; ? \; \frac{5}{6} \longrightarrow \frac{4}{6} < \frac{5}{6}$$

Note: If you would prefer not to teach your student about inequalities at this stage, simply ask them to circle the bigger fraction.

F-15: Word Problems

Here are some word problems your student could try:

1. Samir ate $^5/_8$ of a pizza and Nola ate $^1/_4$. What fraction of the pizza was eaten?

2. On Monday, Mike ran for $1/4$ hour in the morning and $1/2$ hour in the afternoon. What fraction of an hour did Mike run on Monday?

3. Over one supper hour, Yen used $1/2$ of a container of tomatoes, and $1/6$ of a container of olives. How many containers of toppings did he use?

Give your students other questions of this sort.

Sections F-16 to F-20, below, may be taught before or after you give your student the Advanced Fractions Test on page 113.

The Development of Concepts

As your students master the operations in this unit, teach them to articulate the general principles underlying the operations.

You might, for instance, eventually write out simple phrases on their homework that they should be able to repeat and explain.

For example:
- To add two fractions with the same denominator, you just add the numerators (you are adding up the number of pieces).
- The denominator stays the same because it tells you how many pieces the pies are cut into (the piece size).
- The bigger the denominator, the more pieces in the pie, so the smaller the piece.
- When the denominators are different, you must change one or both before you can add the fractions.

To help your student remember an operation and articulate how it works, the following exercise is very effective:

Write down several examples of the operation in which you have made some errors. For instance, if you have covered section F-6 of the manual you might write,

$$\frac{1}{2} + \frac{1}{5}$$ change both denominators

$$\frac{1}{3} + \frac{1}{6}$$ change both denominators

$$\frac{1}{7} + \frac{1}{7}$$ change one denominator

Ask your student to find your mistakes, and explain what you did wrong. Students enjoy this: they work very hard to find your mistakes (and usually keep reminding you that you made them).

F-16: Models of Fractions

The parts of a fraction are equal shares of a whole thing or set. These shares are most commonly represented by regions of a figure (such as a line, circle, or square), or parts of a set.

The exercises below introduce the notion of equal parts, and present an assortment of models of fractions.

1. Circle the pictures that are *not* good models of one-third.

2. Circle the pictures that are *not* good models of one-fourth. Why are the pictures you circled not good models?

3. Use a ruler to divide each line into equal parts.

   a) 6 equal parts   ————————————————————

   b) 5 equal parts   ———————————————————

   c) 2 equal parts   —————————

4. Use a ruler to divide each box into equal parts.

   a) 3 equal parts

   b) 5 equal parts

   c) 2 equal parts

5. Use a ruler to divide each box into 1 cm² boxes.

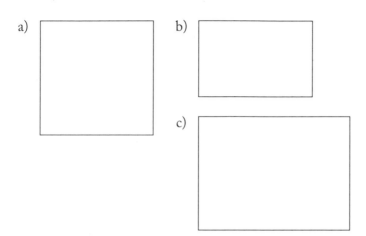

6. What fraction of the following figures are: a) circles? b) squares?

7. What fraction of the following figures are: a) circles? b) squares?
   c) triangles?

8. What fraction of the following figures are: a) grey? b) black?
   c) triangles? d) black circles? e) grey circles? f) black squares?

9. There are five children: $^2/_5$ are boys and $^3/_5$ are girls. Draw a picture showing the girls and boys.

10. What fraction of the edges in the triangle are the same length? (Use a ruler to find the lengths.)

11. What fraction of the edges are on the outside of the figure?

12. What fraction of the squares are on the outside of the figure?

13. A hockey team wins 3 games and loses 2 games.

   a) How many games did the team play?

   b) What fraction of the games did the team win?

   c) Did the team win more than half its games?

14. A hockey team wins 6 games, loses 4 games, and ties 1 game. What fractions of the games did the team . . .

   a) win?

   b) lose?

   c) tie?

15. The chart below shows the number of children in a class with each given hair colour.

Hair Colour	Black	Brown	Red	Blond
Number of Children	7	5	1	3

What fraction of the children have hair that is

a) red?   c) blond?

b) black?   d) brown?

16. A box contains 3 red marbles, 2 blue marbles, and 6 yellow marbles. What fraction of the marbles are *not* red?

F-17: Parts and Wholes

The *denominator* of a fraction indicates the number of pieces in the whole, and the *numerator* the number of pieces being considered. Given a pair of fractions with the same numerator, the fraction with the larger denominator is smaller. Conversely, given a pair of fractions with the same denominator, the fraction with the biggest numerator, is bigger (as it contains more parts). The size of the part of a fraction depends on the size of the whole. The exercises below illustrate several ways of introducing these ideas. You might use concrete materials, such as pattern blocks, to reinforce the idea of fractional size: for instance, your student could use hexagonal and triangular blocks to answer question 11 below.

1. Which fraction has a larger numerator, $^1/_4$ or $^3/_4$? Which fraction is larger? Explain your answer with a picture.

2. Circle the larger fraction in each pair:

$$\frac{3}{5} \text{ or } \frac{4}{5} \qquad \frac{9}{11} \text{ or } \frac{2}{11} \qquad \frac{6}{7} \text{ or } \frac{3}{7}$$

3. Fraction A and fraction B have the same *denominators* (bottoms) but different *numerators* (tops). How can you tell which fraction is larger?

4. Cut the square in half. What fraction of the square is each part? Cut each of the parts in half. What fraction of the square is each new part? As the denominator of the fraction increases, what happens to the size of the piece?

5. Circle the larger fraction in each pair:

$$\frac{1}{3} \text{ or } \frac{1}{7} \qquad \frac{1}{11} \text{ or } \frac{1}{9} \qquad \frac{1}{256} \text{ or } \frac{1}{242}$$

6. Fraction A and fraction B have the same *numerators* (tops), but different *denominators* (bottoms). How can you tell which fraction is larger?

7. Using a ruler, find what fraction of the box is shaded.

a)

b)

c)

8. Each of the lines below is one-third of a line. Use a ruler to draw the *whole* line.

a) ———

b) ——————

9. Using a ruler, complete the figures to make a *whole*.

a) $\dfrac{1}{2}$ b) $\dfrac{1}{3}$ c) $\dfrac{1}{2}$

10. Draw lines from the point in the centre of the hexagon to the vertices of the hexagon. How many triangles cover the hexagon?

11. What fraction of each figure is the shaded part?

12. What fraction of the figure is the shaded piece?

   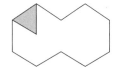

13. The shaded pieces have different shapes. But are they different sizes? Explain your thinking.

14. Is it possible for $\frac{1}{3}$ of a pie to be bigger than $\frac{1}{2}$ of another pie? Show your thinking with a picture.

F-18: Fractions of Sets

Your student should know how to represent a fraction of a set when the denominator of the fraction divides into (but doesn't match) the number of objects in the set.

Exercise 1

For this exercise you will need objects of two different sorts, for instance, red and blue blocks (which are represented below by squares with the letters R and B in them). Have your student carry out the following exercises:

1. Using 2 blocks, make a model of $\frac{1}{2}$. Answer: | R | | B |

2. Using 3 blocks, make a model of $\frac{1}{3}$. Answer: | R | | B | | B |

3. Using 5 blocks, make a model of $\frac{2}{5}$. Answer: | R | | R | | B | | B | | B |

(In all of these questions, the denominator of the fraction matches the number of blocks in the model: make sure your student knows how to build any such model before you go on.)

Now have your student build a model of $\frac{1}{2}$ using 6 blocks as follows:

First, make a model of $\frac{1}{2}$ using the number of blocks given by the denominator of the fraction (in this case, 2). Make sure there is some space between the blocks:

| R | | B |

Think of the red and blue blocks as position markers: you are allowed to add 1 block at a time, to each position, until you have 6 blocks all together (the blocks added must match the colour of the position).

Add 1 block to each position:

| R | | R | | B | | B |

Add another block to each position:

| R | R | R |

| B | B | B |

The procedure stops at this point, as the model contains 6 blocks.

Here is another example: Build a model of $1/3$ using 12 blocks.

First, build a model of $1/3$ using 3 blocks (that is, using the number of blocks given by the denominator):

| R |

| B |

| B |

Now continue adding blocks to the positions until you have 12 blocks:

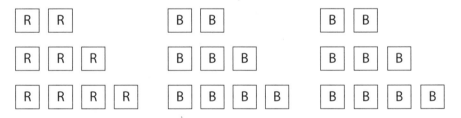

Push the blocks in each position together to show that 12 has been divided into three equal parts, or thirds:

| R | R | R | R | | B | B | B | B | | B | B | B | B |

Your student should see that $1/3$ is equal to $4/12$. Also, point out that the number of blocks in each position (4) is equal to the total number of blocks (12) divided by the denominator of the fraction (3). One-third of 12 is 4.

Allow your student enough practice building models that they can answer questions of the following sort without the model:

Suppose you were to build a model of $^2/_5$ using 20 blocks.

- How many positions would you start with? Answer: 5 positions. (This is just the denominator of the fraction.)
- How many of the starting positions would be red? Answer: 2 positions. (This is just the numerator of the fraction.)
- How many blocks would you place in each position? Answer: 4. (Divide the total number of blocks in the model by the number of positions.)
- How many blocks in your model would be red? Answer: 8. (There are 2 red positions, with 4 blocks in each position.)

Exercise 2
This exercise gives another way of visualising cases where the denominator of the fraction divides the total number of objects.

Start with the following questions:

1. Shade $^1/_3$ of the boxes.

2. Shade $^2/_5$ of the boxes.

3. Shade $^7/_{10}$ of the boxes.

Make sure your student understands that these questions are easy because the denominator matches the number of boxes; the number of boxes you shade is simply the numerator of the fraction.

Now show your student how to shade $^3/_5$ of 10 boxes as follows:

Step 1. Divide the number of boxes by the denominator of the fraction:

$$10 \div 5 = 2$$

Step 2. Multiply the top and bottom of the fraction by the answer from the previous step:

$$\frac{2 \times 3}{2 \times 5} = \frac{6}{10}$$

The idea in this step is to make the denominator of the fraction match the number of boxes. Once you have changed the fraction, you can see immediately how many boxes you should shade — it's just the numerator of the new fraction: i.e., you shade 6 boxes:

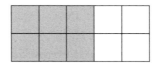

Give your student practice with questions of the following sort: Shade $^2/_3$ of 9 boxes; shade $^1/_4$ of 12 boxes; etc. You might also draw arrays of dots and have them circle fractions of the arrays, for instance:

Circle $^2/_3$ of the dots:

● ● ●
● ● ●

You might also give your student questions where they have to deal with more than one fraction, for instance:

Colour $\frac{1}{4}$ of the boxes red, $\frac{3}{5}$ blue, $\frac{1}{10}$ green, and $\frac{1}{20}$ yellow. (In this case, they must change all the denominators to 20.)

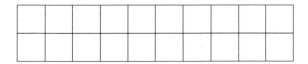

Here are some more questions your student could try:

1. Draw 12 boxes. Colour $\frac{1}{3}$ red, $\frac{1}{4}$ blue and $\frac{5}{12}$ yellow.

2. Draw 8 boxes. Colour $\frac{1}{2}$ red, $\frac{1}{4}$ blue and $\frac{1}{4}$ yellow.

F-19: Fractions of Whole Numbers

Teach your student how to find fractions of whole numbers in their head.

Example: Find $\frac{2}{5}$ of 15.

Step 1. Divide the whole number by the denominator of the fraction:

$$15 \div 5 = 3$$

Step 2. Multiply the top and bottom of the fraction by your answer from the last step:

$$\frac{3 \times 2}{3 \times 5} = \frac{6}{15}$$

Step 3. The numerator of the new fraction is the answer to the question:

$$6 \quad \text{is} \quad \frac{2}{5} \quad \text{of} \quad 15$$

If your student wants to take a shortcut, they can simply multiply the numerator by the result of dividing the whole number by the denominator:

$$2 \quad \times \quad (15 \div 5) \quad = \quad 6$$

Here are some questions your student could try:

1. Find $^3/_5$ of 10.

2. Find $^3/_4$ of 12.

3. Find $^4/_5$ of 25

F-20: Equivalent Fractions

Your student should also be able to solve the following equivalence problems by looking at the pictures:

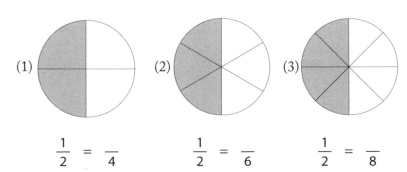

(1) $\dfrac{1}{2} = \dfrac{}{4}$ (2) $\dfrac{1}{2} = \dfrac{}{6}$ (3) $\dfrac{1}{2} = \dfrac{}{8}$

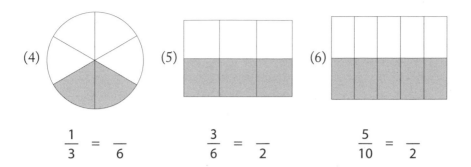

(4) $\dfrac{1}{3} = \dfrac{}{6}$

(5) $\dfrac{3}{6} = \dfrac{}{2}$

(6) $\dfrac{5}{10} = \dfrac{}{2}$

Your student should also be able to answer these questions:

1. Name a fraction equivalent to a whole pie.

2. Draw and shade $\frac{1}{2}$ a pie. By cutting the shaded and unshaded pieces into smaller pieces, find a fraction equivalent to $\frac{1}{2}$. (Repeat this question with $\frac{1}{3}$.)

Tell your student that when they multiply the numerator and denominator of a fraction by a given number, say 2, they should simply imagine cutting each piece of a pie representing the fraction into two pieces.

For instance,

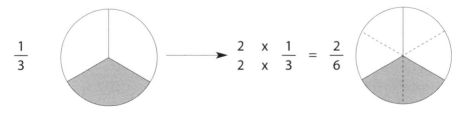

$\dfrac{1}{3}$ $\qquad\longrightarrow\qquad$ $\dfrac{2 \times 1}{2 \times 3} = \dfrac{2}{6}$

To add a pair of fractions with different denominators, you must cut both pies into the same number of pieces (see the picture of $^1/_2$ + $^1/_3$ in section F-4). For instance,

$$\frac{1}{2} + \frac{1}{4} = \frac{2 \times 1}{2 \times 2} + \frac{1}{4} = \frac{2}{4} + \frac{1}{4}$$

Here, you are cutting each piece in the first pie into two pieces, to give four pieces all together.

Show this with a picture:

Note on the Advanced Fractions Test

JUMP students who complete sections F-1 to F-15 of the fractions unit must score 80% or higher on the Advanced Fractions Test before they move on to new units. The Advanced Fractions Test does not completely test a student's understanding of fractions. The point of the test is largely psychological: students who learn to perform complex calculations with fractions, and who do well on the test, show remarkable improvements in confidence, concentration, and numerical ability. This has been demonstrated in 50 elementary classrooms, with more than 1000 students.

The concepts underlying fractions are introduced more fully in sections F-16 to F-20 of the fractions unit (and also in the Fractions II unit of *The JUMP Teaching Manual*).

The Advanced Fractions Test

1. Name these fractions:

a)

b)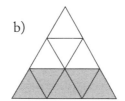

2. Add or subtract:

a) $\dfrac{1}{5} + \dfrac{2}{5} =$

b) $\dfrac{3}{9} + \dfrac{2}{9} =$

c) $\dfrac{7}{11} + \dfrac{2}{11} =$

d) $\dfrac{2}{3} + \dfrac{1}{2} =$

e) $\dfrac{1}{2} + \dfrac{1}{10} =$

f) $\dfrac{3}{4} - \dfrac{1}{5} =$

g) $\dfrac{2}{3} - \dfrac{1}{12} =$

h) $\dfrac{1}{3} + \dfrac{1}{5} + \dfrac{1}{15} =$

3. Reduce:

a) $\dfrac{5}{25} =$

b) $\dfrac{6}{9} =$

c) $\dfrac{4}{12} =$

d) $\dfrac{25}{35} =$

4. Convert to an improper fraction:

   a) $3\dfrac{2}{5} =$ b) $2\dfrac{3}{4} =$

5. Convert to a mixed fraction:

   a) $\dfrac{9}{2} =$ b) $\dfrac{14}{3} =$

6. Add:

   a) $1\dfrac{3}{4} + 3\dfrac{1}{3} =$ b) $2\dfrac{1}{2} + \dfrac{1}{6} =$

7. Circle the larger fraction in each pair:

   a) $\dfrac{1}{2}$ $\dfrac{3}{5}$ b) $\dfrac{2}{5}$ $\dfrac{12}{20}$

8. Samira ate $^1/_4$ of a pizza and Tom ate $^5/_8$. What fraction of a pizza did they eat?

CHAPTER 7

Multiplication and Division

M-1: Multiplication as a Short Form of Addition

Your student should know that multiplication is a short form, or abbreviation, for addition. For instance, 3 x 5 = 5 + 5 + 5. The statement 3 x 5 can also be interpreted as 3 + 3 + 3 + 3 + 3, but you can explain this when your student is more familiar with the concept of multiplication. In the beginning, always have your student write the addition statement using the second number in the given product.

Have your student write various multiplication statements as addition statements. For instance:

3   x   2   =   2   +   2   +   2

4   x   3   =   ?

5   x   2   =   ?

Your student should also know how to represent a multiplication statement with an array of dots. For instance, 3 x 5 can be represented as 3 *rows* of 5 dots:

$$
\begin{array}{ccccc}
\bullet & \bullet & \bullet & \bullet & \bullet \\
\bullet & \bullet & \bullet & \bullet & \bullet \\
\bullet & \bullet & \bullet & \bullet & \bullet \\
\end{array}
$$

Have your student draw arrays for the following statements (make sure the number of rows matches the first number in the statement, and the number of dots in each row matches the second number).

(1) 2 x 5   (2) 3 x 3   (3) 4 x 6

Your student should know how to draw arrays to represent statements that involve addition *and* multiplication. For instance,

3 x 5 + 2 x 5

may be represented by

$$= (3 + 2) \times 5 = 5 \times 5$$

Your student should see from the array that

3 x 5 + 2 x 5 = (3 + 2) x 5

(This is the distributive law.)

Have your student draw arrays for:

(1) 2 x 2 + 3 x 2   (2) 3 x 4 + 2 x 4   (3) 4 x 5 + 2 x 5

If your student seems confident about multiplication, you could point out that 3 x 5 can be represented as 3 rows of 5 dots *or* 5 rows of 3 dots: in either representation, one still has the same number of dots. Hence, in translating a multiplication statement into an addition statement, one may use either the first or the second number: e.g., 3 x 5 = 5 + 5 + 5 *or* 3 + 3 + 3 + 3 + 3.

From this, it is easy to see that multiplication commutes, i.e., it doesn't matter what order you write the numbers in (3 x 5 = 5 x 3).

Finally, tell your student that knowing their times tables will help them solve problems that would otherwise require a good deal of work adding up numbers. For instance, have them solve the following problems by multiplying:

1. There are 4 pencils in a box. How many pencils are there in 5 boxes?

2. A stool has 3 legs. How many legs would 6 stools have?

3. A boat can hold 2 people. How many people can 7 boats hold?

(See section M-3 for more complicated problems of this sort.)

M-2: Understanding Multiplication and Division via Sets

Show your student how to divide a number into *groups* or *sets*.

Example: Divide 10 into sets of 2.

Step 1: Draw 10 lines:

| | | | | | | | | |

Step 2: Draw boxes around each group of 2:

[| |] [| |] [| |] [| |] [| |]

Have your student say out loud, "10 divided into groups of 2 is 5," and then write a division statement:

10 ÷ 2 = 5

Using boxes (for sets or groups) have your student divide:

(1) 6 into groups of 2   (2) 12 into sets of 3   (3) 9 into groups of 3

To write a division statement based on a picture, your student should write the total number of lines divided by the number of lines in each box equals the number of boxes, e.g., dividing 12 into sets of 3 gives 4 sets:

[| | |] [| | |] [| | |] [| | |]

12 ÷ 3 = 4

Your student should also be aware that there is another way to interpret the picture: dividing 12 into 4 parts (or sets) gives 3 objects in each set. Hence, they could also write:

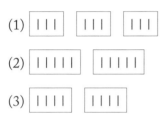

12 ÷ 4 = 3

Have your student write two division statements for each of the following pictures:

(1) | | | | | | | | |

(2) | | | | | | | | | |

(3) | | | | | | | |

Have your student write *multiplication* statements for the pictures above as follows: the number of boxes times the number of lines in each box equals the total number of lines.

M-3: Understanding Multiplication and Division via Sets (cont'd)

A student will find word problems involving multiplication and division easy if they are familiar with the notion of a set (or group) of objects or things.

A box can be used to represent a set, and lines to represent the objects in each set. Make sure your student understands that the lines could stand for anything: pencils in a box, people in a boat, or legs on a dog. Ask your student to fill in the blanks in questions of the following sort:

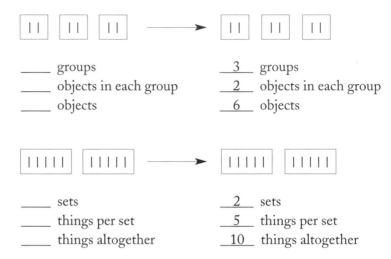

_____ groups   __3__ groups
_____ objects in each group   __2__ objects in each group
_____ objects   __6__ objects

_____ sets   __2__ sets
_____ things per set   __5__ things per set
_____ things altogether   __10__ things altogether

When you are sure your student is completely familiar with the terms "set," "group," and "per" (which means "for every," or "in each"), and you are certain that they understand the difference between the phrases "objects in each group," and "objects" (or "objects all together," or "objects in total"), have them write a description of the diagrams themselves, for example:

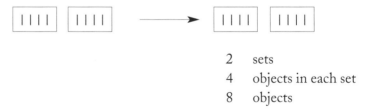

2   sets
4   objects in each set
8   objects

There are three types of word problems involving multiplication and division.

Type 1: You know the number of sets and the number of objects in each set.

Example: You have 4 sets of objects and 2 objects in each set. How many objects do you have in total?

Draw 4 boxes to represent the 4 sets:

Fill each box with 2 objects:

Count the number of objects:

8 objects (or "8 objects all together" or "8 objects in total")

Ask your student to write a multiplication statement to represent the solution:

4   x   2   =   8

Give your student practice with questions of the following sort:

(1) 3 sets
    5 objects
    How many objects?

(2) 3 groups
    7 objects in each group
    How many objects in total?

Type 2: You know how many objects there are all together and how many objects there are in each set.

Example: You have 6 objects all together and 3 objects in each set. How many sets do you have?

Draw the total number of objects:

| | | | | | |

Put three objects at a time into a box until you've put all the objects in boxes:

| | | | | | | |

Count the number of boxes:

2 boxes (or sets)

Ask your student to write a division statement representing the solution:

6 ÷ 3 = 2

Give your student practice with questions of the following sort:

(1) 12 objects all together (2) 16 objects
4 objects in each set 2 objects per set
How many sets? How many sets?

Type 3: You know how many objects and how many sets there are.

Example: You have 10 objects and 5 sets. How many objects are there in each set?

Draw the total number of sets:

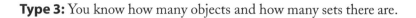

Put one object in each set:

Check to see if you have placed all 10 objects. If not, put one more object in each set. Continue until you have placed all the objects:

Count the number of objects in each set:

2 objects in each set

Ask your student to write a division statement to represent the solution:

10 ÷ 5 = 2

M-4: Word Problems Involving Multiplication and Division

When your student is able to distinguish between and solve problems of types 1, 2, and 3 readily, you can teach them how to solve more general word problems involving multiplication and division. Tell them to think of a container (like a box or pot) or a carrier (like a car or a boat) as a set, and the things contained or carried as the objects.

Example: 10 people need to cross a river. A boat can hold 2 people. How many boats are needed to take everyone across?

Think of the boats as sets (or boxes) and the people as objects placed in the sets. This is a problem of type 2 (you know the total number of objects and the number of objects in each set).

Draw 10 lines to represent 10 people:

| | | | | | | | | | |

Put boxes around every 2 lines (each box represents a boat):

Count the number of boats:

5 boats

This approach also works for things that have parts (think of the things that have parts as sets, and the parts as objects in the set).

Example: A cat has 2 eyes. How many eyes are there on 5 cats?

Use boxes to represent each cat and lines in each box to represent the eyes. This is a problem of type 1 (you know the number of sets and the number of objects in each set).

Draw 5 boxes to represent the 5 cats:

Draw 2 lines in each box (representing the eyes):

Count the number of lines to give you the answer:

10 eyes

This approach also works for things that have a *value* or a *price* (think of the thing with value as a set or box, and the price or value as the objects in the set, e.g., you can think of dollars or cents as lines that you can place inside the box representing the thing you are buying).

Example: A piece of gum costs 5 cents. You have 15 cents. How many pieces of gum can you buy?

This is a problem of type 2.

Draw 15 lines to represent 15 cents:

| | | | | | | | | | | | | | |

Put boxes around every 5 lines (each box represents a piece of gum):

| | | | | | | | | | | | | | | | | |

Count the number of boxes:

3 boxes or pieces of gum

If you give your student enough practice with this type of problem, eventually they should see that they simply have to divide 15 by 5 to find the answer. For sample problems, see worksheet M-4A, starting on page 137.

Worksheet • Multiplication and Division • M-1A

1. Write the following multiplication statements as addition statements:

    a) 3 x 2 =   b) 4 x 2 =   c) 3 x 3 =

    d) 4 x 3 =   e) 2 x 4 =   f) 5 x 3 =

    g) 3 x 5 =   h) 5 x 5 =   i) 3 x 6 =

2. Draw arrays for the following statements:

    a) 3 x 2   b) 3 x 5

    c) 2 x 5   d) 2 x 4

    e) 4 x 5   f) 3 x 6

3. Draw arrays for the following statements:

a) 3 x 3 + 2 x 3

b) 2 x 5 + 2 x 5

c) 4 x 3 + 3 x 3

4. Write a multiplication statement for the following problems:

a) How many legs   b) How many fingers   c) How many eyes
on 3 chairs?   on 4 hands?   on 5 lions?

Worksheet • Multiplication and Division • M-2A

1. Using lines and boxes divide:

    a) 6 into groups of 2   b) 12 into sets of 4

    c) 10 into groups of 5   d) 10 into groups of 2

    e) 9 into groups of 3   f) 8 into sets of 2

2. Write two division statements for each of the following pictures:

    a) | | | | | |

    b) | | | | | | | | | | | | | | |

    c) | | | |

    d) | | | | | | | | | | | |

    e) | | | | | | | | | | | |

3. Draw circles to divide these arrays into:

a) groups of 2

• • •
• • •

b) groups of 3

• • •
• • •

c) groups of 3

• • • •
• • • •
• • • •

d) groups of 4

• • • •
• • • •
• • • •

e) groups of 2

• • • • •
• • • • •

f) groups of 5

• • • • •
• • • • •

g) groups of 3

• • • • •
• • • • •
• • • • •

h) groups of 5

• • • • •
• • • • •
• • • • •

Now go back and write two division statements for each picture.

BONUS

For each picture, write two *division* statements and a *multiplication* statement.

a) | | | | | | | | | | | |

b) | | | | | | | |

c) | | | | | | | | | |

Worksheet • Multiplication and Division • M-3A

1. Fill in the blanks:

a) | | | | | | | |

_____ sets
_____ objects in each set
_____ objects

b) | | | | | | | | |

_____ sets
_____ objects in each set
_____ objects

c) | | | | | | | | | |

_____ sets
_____ objects in each set
_____ objects altogether

d) | | | | | | | | | | | |

_____ groups
_____ things in each group
_____ things altogether

e) | | | | | | | | | | | |

_____ sets
_____ things in each set
_____ things in total

2. State the number of sets, the number of objects in each set, and the total number of objects:

a)

b) | | | | | | | | | | | | | | |

c) | | | | | | | | | | | |

d) | | | | | | | | | |

e) | | | | | | | | | |

f) | | | | | | | | | | | | | | | |

3. Draw a picture, using boxes for sets and lines for objects, to show how many *objects* there are *in total*. Then write a multiplication statement.

a) 3 sets of objects
   2 objects in each set

b) 5 sets of objects
   2 objects in each set

c) 4 sets
   3 objects in each set

d) 4 objects in each set
   3 sets

e) 3 groups of objects
   3 objects per group

f) 3 objects per set
   5 sets

4. Using boxes and lines, show how many *sets* you need. Then write
   a division statement.

   a) 6 objects in total
       3 objects in each set

   b) 10 objects in total
       2 objects per set

   c) 3 objects per set
       9 objects all together

5. Using boxes and lines, show how many *objects* are *in each set*. Then write a division statement.

a) 6 objects in total
   3 objects in each set

b) 10 objects in total
   2 objects per set

c) 3 objects per set
   9 objects all together

6. Use a drawing to solve each of the following:

a) 6 objects in total
   3 sets
   How many objects in each set?

b) 3 objects in each set
   15 objects
   How many sets?

c) 4 objects in each set
   5 sets
   How many objects?

Worksheet • Word Problems • M-4A

1. To solve each question, think of containers or carriers as *sets*, and the people or things carried or contained as *objects*. Use boxes and lines in your answers.

a) 3 cars
   2 people in each car
   How many people?

b) 20 people
   5 boats
   How many people in each boat?

c) 5 plates
   3 cookies on each plate
   How many cookies?

d) 20 pens
   4 pens in each box
   How many boxes?

e) 2 buses
   6 people on each bus
   How many people?

f) 15 flowers
   5 flowers in each pot
   How many pots?

2. To solve these problems, think of things that have parts as *sets*, and think of the parts as *objects* in the set.

a) 5 chairs
   4 legs per chair
   How many legs?

b) 16 legs
   4 legs per chair
   How many chairs?

c) 3 wheels per bicycle
   5 bicycles
   How many wheels?

d) 2 ears on each cat
   10 ears
   How many cats?

e) 3 spots on each dog
   15 spots
   How many dogs?

f) 5 fingers on a hand
   20 fingers
   How many hands?

3. To solve the following problems, think of rows as *sets* and chairs as *objects*. Draw a picture to show your answer.

a) 5 rows
   3 chairs in each row
   How many chairs?

b) 10 chairs
   2 rows
   How many chairs in each row?

c) 3 chairs in each row
   15 chairs
   How many rows?

4. Think of things that have value, or cost money, as *sets*, and the cost of each thing as the number of *objects* in each set. (Use lines and boxes.)

a) 5 tickets
   4 dollars for each ticket
   How many dollars do the tickets cost?

b) 5 cents for each piece of gum
   You paid 20 cents
   How many pieces of gum did you buy?

c) You paid 12 dollars
   You bought 4 cups
   How much did each cup cost?

5. Write a multiplication or division statement to solve each of the following:

    a) 4 objects in each set
       16 objects in total
       How many sets?

    b) 25 objects in total
       5 sets
       How many objects per set?

    c) 3 sets
       4 objects per set
       How many objects?

6. Write a multiplication or division statement for each of the following:

    a) 5 cats
       3 fleas on each cat
       How many fleas?

    b) 12 birds
       3 birds in each tree
       How many trees?

    c) 4 bowls
       3 fish in each bowl
       How many fish?

CHAPTER 8

Coordinate Systems

CO-1: Introducing Coordinates

To illustrate the idea of a coordinate system, you can start with the following card trick. Deal out nine cards, face up, in the arrangement shown in the picture.

Row 3

Row 2

Row 1

Column 1   Column 2   Column 3

Tell your student that to perform the trick they must be able to identify the *rows* and *columns* of the array: the columns run vertically and the rows run horizontally. In mathematical applications, the columns of an array are often numbered in increasing order from right to left and the rows are numbered in increasing order from bottom to top (as shown in the picture).

Positions in the array are identified by a column number, followed by a row number. For instance, the position marked with an X in the diagram is in column 2, row 3. Give your student a column number and a row number and ask them to identify the card in that position in your array. Repeat this until your student can quickly find any position (you might use larger arrays, too). Then point to a card and ask your student to tell you its column number and row number. Repeat this until your student can name any position. (Make sure your student knows that they should always name the column first, then the row, and that the rows are numbered in increasing order *from the bottom up*, as in the figure above.)

Tell your student that positions in an array can be represented by dots, and that as a short form the column number and row number can be represented by an ordered pair of numbers in a bracket. For instance, column 1, row 3 can be written (1,3). The first number in the bracket always represents the column and the second, the row. (For practice, see worksheet CO-1A, exercise 1.)

Your student should understand that different ways of identifying positions might be used: letters might be used instead of numbers, the numbering might start with 0 rather than 1 (as in exercise 2 on worksheet CO-1A), or the rows might be numbered in increasing order from the top down. Your student should be aware, however, that in all of the applications in this unit, rows are numbered in increasing order from the bottom up.

Finally, your student should understand that a set of positions needn't always be represented by an array of dots or rectangles. The most useful way to indicate position is to use a grid of vertical and horizontal lines, or a graph (see exercise 3 on worksheet CO-1A). On a graph, the positions are the points where the vertical lines (the columns) meet the horizontal lines (the rows).

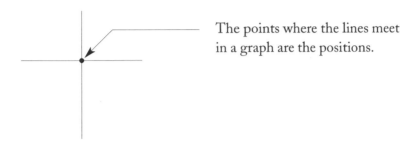

The points where the lines meet in a graph are the positions.

The ordered pairs A (1,3), B (4,2), and C (0,0) represent points located at the positions shown on the graph below:

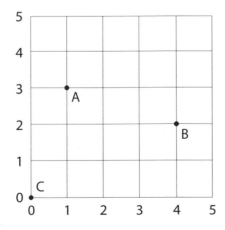

Sample questions for graphing are given in exercise 3 of worksheet CO-1A. If your student wonders why the numbers on the graph start at 0 rather than 1, tell them that graphs are normally used to represent the position of things relative to a particular starting point. For example, in the map on page 153, the house is placed in the lower left corner of the graph. If you assign this point coordinates (0,0), then the ordered pair associated with the school (3,1) tells you exactly how many blocks you need to travel from the house to get to the school (3 blocks east and 1 block north). That is why it is convenient to give the starting point coordinates (0,0). This point is called the "origin" of the graph.

Your student should also be able to tell you how many rows and how many columns there are in an array. For instance, the following array has two columns and three rows.

$$\begin{matrix} \bullet & \bullet \\ \bullet & \bullet \\ \bullet & \bullet \end{matrix}$$

When your student has finished worksheet CO-1A, tell them that they are now prepared to understand and perform the card trick.

Ask your student to select a card in the array, then tell you what column it's in, but not the card. Gather up the cards, with the three cards in the column your student selected on the top of the deck. Deal the cards face up in another 3 x 3 array making sure the top three cards of the deck end up in the top row of the array. Ask your student to tell you what column their card is in. The top card in that column is their card, which you can now identify. Repeat the trick several times and ask your student to try to figure out how it works. You might give them hints by telling them to watch how you place the cards, or even by repeating the trick with a 2 x 2 array.

When your student understands how the trick works, you can ask the following questions:

1. Would there be any point to the trick if the subject told the person performing the trick both the row and the column number of the card they had selected?

   Clearly there would be no trick if the performer knew both numbers. Two pieces of information are enough to identify unambiguously a position in an array or graph. This is why graphs are such an efficient means of representation: two numbers can identify any location in two-dimensional space (in other words, on a flat sheet of paper). This discovery, made over 300 years ago by the French mathematician René Descartes, was one of the simplest and most revolutionary steps in the history of mathematics and science. His idea of representing position using numbers underlies a great deal of modern mathematics, science, and technology.

   You might ask your student how many numbers would be required to represent the position of an object relative to an origin in three-dimensional space. (The answer is three. Think of the origin as being situated on a plane or flat piece of paper that has a grid or graph on it. You need two numbers to tell you how to travel from the origin along the grid lines on the plane to situate yourself directly above or below the object, and one more number to tell you how far you have to travel up or down from the plane to reach the object.)

2. Would the trick work with a larger array?

   Have them try the trick with a 4 x 4 array. They should see that as long as the array is square (with an equal number of rows and columns), the trick works for any number of cards. Ask your student to explain why this is so and why the trick doesn't work if the array isn't square (for instance, try it with 2 columns and 6 rows).

The trick can be modified for non-square arrays if you allow one extra rearrangement. Deal out an array of 3 columns, 9 rows. Have your student select a card and tell you what column it's in. Re-deal the cards so that the nine cards from the chosen column land in the top three rows of the new array. Ask your student to tell you what column their card is in, and re-deal the top three cards in that column into the top row of a new array. Once your student tells you what column their card is in, you can identify the top card in that column as the one they selected.

This version of the trick illustrates a powerful general principle in science and mathematics: when you are looking for a solution to a problem, it is often possible to eliminate a great many possibilities by asking a well-formulated question. In the card trick above, one is able to single out one of 27 possibilities by asking only three questions. Repeat the trick, asking your student how many possibilities were eliminated by the first question (18), by the second question (6), and by the third (2).

3. Ask your student if the original trick (i.e., with a square array) would work if the subject told the performer which row the card was in rather than which column.

Have your student show you how the new trick would be performed. The fact that the trick works equally well in both cases illustrates a very deep principle of invariance in mathematics. In a square array, there is no real difference between the rows and columns. In fact, if you rotate the array by a quarter turn, the rows become columns and vice versa. More generally, once you fix an origin in space, it doesn't matter how you set up your grid (the lines representing the rows and columns). In all cases, you need only two numbers to identify a position.

CO-2: Graphing

More sample questions for graphing are given on worksheet CO-2A. Before your student tries question 2, make sure they can define and draw a square, a rectangle, a triangle, a parallelogram (a figure with opposite sides equal in length, or equivalently, parallel), and a polygon (a figure with any number of straight sides, not necessarily the same length; a square, a rectangle, a triangle, a parallelogram, a pentagon, and a hexagon are all examples of polygons).

CO-3: Relative Position

On worksheet CO-3A, you'll find exercises that will help your student learn how to describe the position of one point in relation to another.

Your student should be aware that in question 3 of worksheet CO-3A, the letters and numbers have been placed along the edges of the grid (rather than at points of the grid as in previous excercises) and hence identify entire squares (rather than points).

Worksheet • Coordinate Systems • CO-1A

1. Circle the points in the following positions:

a)
```
•   •   •
•   •   •
•   •   •
```
Column 1,
Row 2

b)
```
•   •   •
•   •   •
•   •   •
```
Column 2,
Row 3

c)
```
•   •   •
•   •   •
•   •   •
```
Column 3,
Row 1

d)
```
•   •   •
•   •   •
•   •   •
```
Column 2,
Row 2

e)
```
•   •   •
•   •   •
•   •   •
```
(1,1)

f)
```
•   •   •
•   •   •
•   •   •
```
(3,3)

g)
```
•   •   •
•   •   •
•   •   •
```
(1,3)

h)
```
•   •   •
•   •   •
•   •   •
```
(3,2)

2. Circle the points in the following positions:

a) 3 •   •   •
    2 •   •   •
    1 •   •   •
       A   B   C

       (A,2)

b) C •   •   •
    B •   •   •
    A •   •   •
       X   Y   Z

       (Y,C)

c) 2 •   •   •
    1 •   •   •
    0 •   •   •
       0   1   2

       (0,2)

d) 2 •   •   •
    1 •   •   •
    0 •   •   •
       0   1   2

       (2,0)

3. Put points at the following positions. Label each point with the letter written beside the ordered pair.

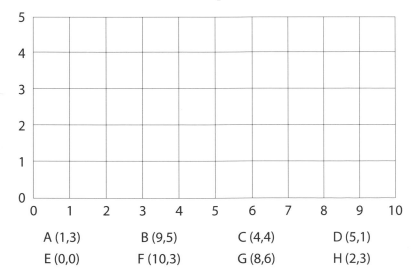

A (1,3)   B (9,5)   C (4,4)   D (5,1)
E (0,0)   F (10,3)   G (8,6)   H (2,3)

Worksheet • Coordinate Systems • CO-2A

1. Write the coordinates of the following points:

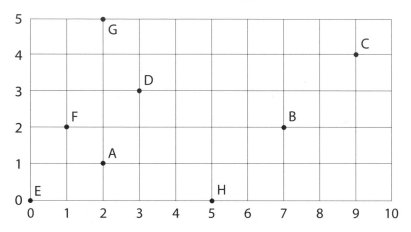

A (,   )   B (,   )

C (,   )   D (,   )

E (,   )   F (,   )

G (,   )   H (,   )

2. Graph each set of ordered pairs and join the dots to form polygons.
   Identify each polygon.

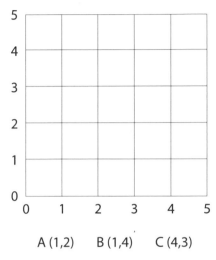

A (1,2)   B (1,4)   C (4,3)

This polygon is a _____

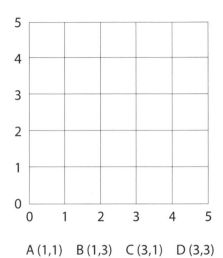

A (1,1)   B (1,3)   C (3,1)   D (3,3)

This polygon is a _____

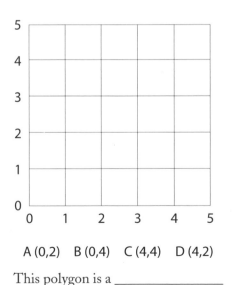

A (0,2)   B (0,4)   C (4,4)   D (4,2)

This polygon is a _____

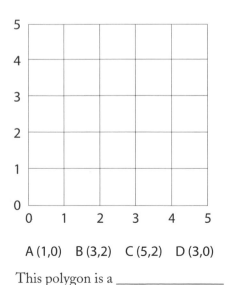

A (1,0)   B (3,2)   C (5,2)   D (3,0)

This polygon is a _____

Worksheet • Coordinate Systems • CO-3A

1.

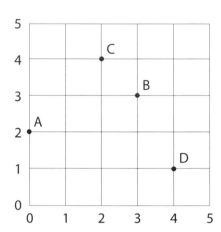

a) What point is 2 right and 2 up from A? _____

b) What point is 4 left and 1 up from D? _____

c) What point is 1 down and 1 right of C? _____

d) Describe how to get from point B to point D:

_____

e) Describe how to go to point B from point A:

_____

f) Describe how to get to point A from point C:

_____

2.

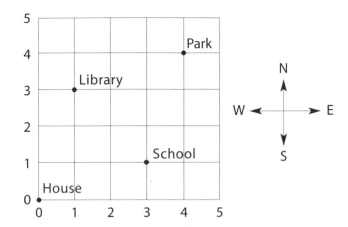

a) What building is 1 block east
   and 3 blocks north of the house? _____

b) What building is 2 blocks west
   and 2 blocks north of the school? _____

c) What building is 1 block south
   and 3 blocks west of the school? _____

d) Describe how to get from the park to the school:

   _____

e) Describe how to go to the library from the school:

   _____

f) Describe how to go to the park from the library:

   _____

3.

4				City	
3	Lake				
2			Moun-tain		Swamp
1					
	A	B	C	D	E

Each square represents a square km.

a) What would you find in square (A,3)? _____

b) What would you find if you
    travelled 2 km west of the swamp? _____

c) Give the coordinates of the city: (,   )

d) Describe how to get from the city to the lake:

    _____

e) Describe how to get from the mountain to the city:

    _____

4.

Sahar		Zoltan	
	Anna		Alan
Yen		Tom	

Use the clues to find where the following children sit:

a) Walk 2 desks down and 1 desk right from Zoltan to find John's seat.

b) Samir is one desk left of Alan.

c) Sally is between Sahar and Zoltan.

d) Walk 2 desks left and 1 desk up from Tom to find Mary's desk.

e) Tara is one desk right of Zoltan.

f) Noor is between Yen and Tom.

CHAPTER 9

Ratios and Percents

Section RP-1: Ratios

A ratio is a comparison of two numbers.

In the picture, the ratio of circles to squares is 2 to 3. A ratio may be written in *ratio form* (2 : 3) or in *fraction form* ($^2/_3$).

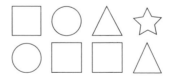

For the diagram above, have your student write, in the ratio form:

    a) The ratio of squares to circles (3 : 2)
    b) The ratio of stars to triangles (1 : 2)
    c) The ratio of circles to stars (2 : 1)
    d) The ratio of triangles to figures (2 : 8)

If your student's reading level is high enough, have them read and answer the following questions (in ratio form):

1. Write the ratio of the number of days in a weekend to the number of days in an entire week.

2. Write the ratio of vowels to consonants in each name:

   a) Toronto   b) Montreal   c) London   d) Paris

3. Write the ratio for the value of a penny to the value of:

   a) a nickel   b) a dime   c) a quarter   d) a dollar

4. Eleven students tried a swimming test. Five passed on the first try. What was the ratio of those passing to those failing?

5. Using this diagram, write the ratios of the lengths:

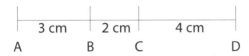

   a) AB to CD   b) BC to AB   c) CD to AC   d) BC to AC

Note: If your student can't read the questions, you might read them aloud and help your student answer the easier ones.

RP-2: Writing Ratios in Lowest Terms

Ratios, like fractions, may be written in lowest terms. If there are 4 apples in a bowl and 2 oranges, one may say the ratio of apples to oranges is 4 to 2 or, equivalently, that there are 2 apples to every 1 orange. You could illustrate this for your student with a picture:

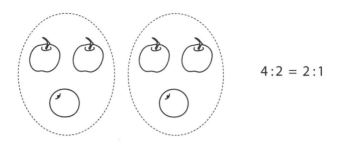

$$4:2 = 2:1$$

Have your student reduce the ratios as follows:

$$2:6 \longrightarrow 2^{\div 2}:6^{\div 2} \longrightarrow 1:3$$

Find a number that divides both terms in the ratio and write a division statement.

Do the division.

Other examples:

$$20:25 \longrightarrow 20^{\div 5}:25^{\div 5} \longrightarrow 4:5$$

$$9:6 \longrightarrow 9^{\div 3}:6^{\div 3} \longrightarrow 3:2$$

Ask your student to reduce these ratios to the lowest terms:

(1) 2:4   (2) 3:6   (3) 5:10   (4) 5:20   (5) 2:10

(6) 8:2   (7) 9:3   (8) 4:6   (9) 20:25   (10) 12:15

If your student knows other times tables, make up ratios divisible by numbers other than 2, 3, or 5.

RP-3: Comparing Ratios

If there are 4 apples for every 2 oranges in a bowl, then there are 2 apples for every 1 orange. The ratios 4 : 2 and 2 : 1 are equivalent. To tell whether a pair of ratios is equivalent, you must first reduce each ratio to lowest terms.

Example: Are 6 : 9 and 10 : 15 equivalent ratios?

$$6^{\div 3}:9^{\div 3}=2:3 \qquad\qquad 10^{\div 5}:15^{\div 5}=2:3$$

The ratios reduce to the same ratio, hence they are equivalent.

Example: Are 3 : 1 and 12 : 9 equivalent ratios?

$$12^{\div 3}:9^{\div 3}=4:3$$

3 : 1 is already reduced to lowest terms and does not equal 4 : 3, hence the ratios are not equivalent.

Have your student reduce the following pairs of ratios to lowest terms and decide whether they are equivalent:

(1) 1 : 3 and 2 : 6   (2) 2 : 3 and 6 : 9   (3) 1 : 2 and 2 : 10

(4) 25 : 5 and 5 : 1   (5) 4 : 6 and 10 : 15 (6) 20 : 25 and 3 : 5

(7) 12 : 15 and 25 : 20 (8) 21 : 7 and 3 : 1   (9) 6 : 8 and 9 : 12

You can make up other examples involving times tables other than 2, 3, and 5. (*Note:* Order matters in ratios — for example, 1 : 3 is not the same ratio as 3 : 1).

RP-4: Solving for Equivalent Ratios or Fractions

In this section, your student will learn how to find the missing number in ratios like:

$$\frac{2}{3} = \frac{6}{\quad} \qquad \text{or} \qquad \frac{\quad}{4} = \frac{15}{20}$$

If you give them lots of practice at the steps below, they should find these questions easy.

Step 1: Find the missing number (multiplication).

$$\underline{5} \xrightarrow{\ \times 3\ } \underline{\quad} \xrightarrow{\hspace{3cm}} \underline{5} \xrightarrow{\ \times 3\ } \underline{15}$$

Multiply the number at
the tail of the arrow by the
number on top of the arrow.

Have your student fill in the missing numbers for these questions:

(1) $\underline{2} \xrightarrow{\ \times 3\ } \underline{\quad}$ (2) $\underline{3} \xrightarrow{\ \times 3\ } \underline{\quad}$

(3) $\underline{5} \xrightarrow{\ \times 3\ } \underline{\quad}$ (4) $\underline{\quad} \xleftarrow{\ \times 3\ } \underline{2}$

(5) $\underline{\quad} \xleftarrow{\ \times 3\ } \underline{4}$ (6) $\underline{\quad} \xleftarrow{\ \times 3\ } \underline{3}$

(In this section and all subsequent sections, you should make up extra questions involving the times tables your student knows.)

Step 2: Find the missing number (division).

$$\_\_ \xrightarrow{\text{x 4}} \underline{20} \xrightarrow{\hspace{3cm}} \underline{5} \xrightarrow{\text{x 4}} \underline{20}$$

Divide the number at
the tip of the arrow by the
number on top of the arrow.

Have your student fill in the missing numbers for these questions:

(1) $\_\_ \xrightarrow{\text{x 4}} \underline{12}$ (2) $\_\_ \xrightarrow{\text{x 2}} \underline{8}$ (3) $\_\_ \xrightarrow{\text{x 5}} \underline{20}$

(4) $\_\_ \xrightarrow{\text{x 3}} \underline{9}$ (5) $\_\_ \xrightarrow{\text{x 4}} \underline{16}$ (6) $\_\_ \xrightarrow{\text{x 2}} \underline{10}$

(7) $\underline{25} \xleftarrow{\text{x 5}} \_\_$ (8) $\underline{6} \xleftarrow{\text{x 3}} \_\_$ (9) $\underline{6} \xleftarrow{\text{x 2}} \_\_$

Step 3: Distinguish between the two cases.

Make sure your student knows that if they are given the number at the
tail of the arrow they multiply, and if at the *tip*, they divide. (You might
have them say out loud, in each case, "tail," or "tip" — make sure they
know the tip is the pointed end, and that they can distinguish between
the tip and the tail no matter which way the arrow is pointing.)

Find the missing numbers:

(1) $\_\_ \xrightarrow{\text{x 2}} \underline{10}$ (2) $\_\_ \xleftarrow{\text{x 3}} \underline{5}$ (3) $\_\_ \xrightarrow{\text{x 5}} \underline{20}$

(4) $\underline{6} \xleftarrow{\text{x 2}} \_\_$ (5) $\underline{12} \xleftarrow{\text{x 4}} \_\_$ (6) $\_\_ \xrightarrow{\text{x 3}} \underline{9}$

(7) $\_\_ \xleftarrow{\text{x 5}} \underline{3}$ (8) $\underline{5} \xrightarrow{\text{x 2}} \_\_$ (9) $\_\_ \xrightarrow{\text{x 5}} \underline{25}$

Also make sure your student knows how to check their answer by multiplying the number at the tail of the arrow by the one on top of the arrow to see if they get the number at the tip. You might make up questions in which you have filled in the wrong answer and have your student find your errors. Your student should be able to solve these arrow problems without any difficulty before you proceed.

Step 4: Filling in the arrows.

Make sure you have your student practise each of these steps individually, if necessary.

$$\frac{3}{4} = \frac{}{12} \longrightarrow \frac{3}{4} \to \frac{}{12} \longrightarrow \frac{3}{4} \xrightarrow{\times 3} \frac{}{12}$$

On the level where both numbers are provided, draw an arrow from the smallest number to the largest.

Write in a times statement.

$$\longrightarrow \frac{3}{4} \overset{\times 3}{\underset{\times 3}{=}} \frac{}{12}$$

Write the same arrow on the other level.

Then solve the arrow problem as in step 3, above.

Here are some other examples:

$$\frac{2}{3} = \frac{6}{} \longrightarrow \frac{2}{3} \xrightarrow{\times 3} \frac{6}{} \longrightarrow \frac{2}{3} \overset{\times 3}{\underset{\times 3}{=}} \frac{6}{} \longrightarrow \frac{2}{3} = \frac{6}{9}$$

$$\frac{20}{25} = \frac{}{5} \longrightarrow \frac{20}{25} \xleftarrow{} 5 \longrightarrow \frac{20}{25} \overset{\times 5}{\underset{\times 5}{\xleftarrow{=}}} 5 \longrightarrow \frac{20}{25} = \frac{4}{5}$$

Now, have your student solve these ratios:

(1) $\dfrac{3}{4} = \dfrac{}{20}$ (2) $\dfrac{4}{5} = \dfrac{}{25}$ (3) $\dfrac{2}{3} = \dfrac{10}{}$ (4) $\dfrac{}{5} = \dfrac{12}{15}$

(5) $\dfrac{25}{30} = \dfrac{}{6}$ (6) $\dfrac{12}{16} = \dfrac{3}{}$ (7) $\dfrac{7}{10} = \dfrac{14}{}$ (8) $\dfrac{5}{3} = \dfrac{25}{}$

To make up a ratio question, start with a pair of equivalent fractions (e.g., $^4/_7 = {}^{12}/_{21}$) then leave one number out ($/_7 = {}^{12}/_{21}$).

Not all ratios can be solved by the arrow method. You can only use the arrow method when the smaller number given divides into the larger. To solve ratios that can't be solved by the arrow method, you must cross-multiply.

Here is an example of cross-multiplication:

$$\dfrac{2}{3} = \dfrac{5}{} \qquad \dfrac{2}{3} = \dfrac{5}{x} \qquad 2x = 15 \qquad x = \dfrac{15}{2}$$

If your student is learning ratios for the first time, stick to questions that can be solved by the arrow method.

If your student is good at long division, you might give them harder questions, such as:

$$\dfrac{3}{5} = \dfrac{}{125}$$

RP-5: Word Problems

Example: There are 3 cats in a pet shop for every 2 dogs. If there are 12 cats in the shop, how many dogs are there?

Step 1: Write, as a fraction, the ratio of the two things being compared:

$$\frac{3}{2}$$

Step 2: Write, in words, what each number stands for:

$$\begin{array}{c} \text{cats} \\ \text{dogs} \end{array} \quad \frac{3}{2}$$

Step 3: On the other side of an equal sign, write the *same* words, on the *same* levels:

$$\begin{array}{c} \text{cats} \\ \text{dogs} \end{array} \quad \frac{3}{2} = \underline{} \quad \begin{array}{c} \text{cats} \\ \text{dogs} \end{array}$$

Step 4: Re-read the question to determine which quantity (i.e., cats or dogs) has been given (in this case, cats) — then place that quantity on the proper level:

$$\begin{array}{c} \text{cats} \\ \text{dogs} \end{array} \quad \frac{3}{2} = \frac{12}{} \quad \begin{array}{c} \text{cats} \\ \text{dogs} \end{array}$$

Step 5: Solve the ratio using the method described in section RP-4.

Here are some questions your student can solve:

1. There are 2 apples in a bowl for every 3 oranges. If there are 9 oranges, how many apples are there?

2. There are 3 boys in a class for every 4 girls. If there are 12 girls in the class, how many boys are there?

3. Five bus tickets cost $3. How many bus tickets can you buy with $9?

4. A basketball team won 2 out of every 3 games they played. They played a total of 15 games. How many games did they win? (*Note:* the quantities are "games won" and "games played.")

5. To make fruit punch, you mix 1 litre of orange juice with 2 litres of pineapple juice. If you have 3 litres of orange juice, how many litres of pineapple juice do you need?

6. Nora can run 3 laps in 4 minutes. At that rate, how many laps could she run in 12 minutes?

7. The ratio of boys to girls in a class is 4 : 5. If there are 20 boys, how many girls are there?

8. The ratio of the top speed of a lion to the top speed of a hyena is 5 : 4. A hyena's top speed is 64 km/hr. What is a lion's top speed?

9. Neptune orbits the sun 3 times in the same time it takes Pluto to orbit the sun 2 times. How many orbits does Pluto complete while Neptune orbits 12 times?

10. 2 cm on a map represents 5 km in real life. If a lake is 6 cm long on the map, what is its actual size? (*Note:* Here the quantities compared are cm and km.)

RP-6: Percents

A percent is a ratio that compares a number to 100. The term "percent" means "out of 100" or "for every 100." For instance, 84% on a test means 84 out of 100. Tell your student that they can think of percent as a short form for a fraction with 100 in the denominator. For example,

$$45\% \quad = \quad \frac{45}{100}$$

Have your student write the following percents as fractions:

(1) 7%   (2) 92%   (3) 5%   (4) 15%   (5) 50%   (6) 100%

Have your student write the following fractions as percents:

(1) $\dfrac{2}{100}$ (2) $\dfrac{31}{100}$ (3) $\dfrac{52}{100}$ (4) $\dfrac{100}{100}$ (5) $\dfrac{7}{100}$ (6) $\dfrac{88}{100}$

RP-7: Converting Simple Fractions to Percents

Have your student memorize the following times tables (they should know them really well):

$$10 \times 10 = 100 \qquad 4 \times 25 = 100 \qquad 5 \times 20 = 100$$

$$2 \times 50 = 100 \qquad 3 \times 25 = 75$$

Also make sure that they can multiply numbers with zeroes on the end, for example,

$$4 \times 20 = 80 \qquad 3 \times 30 = 90$$

Do not proceed until your student can solve the following arrow problems with ease:

(1) 2 $\xrightarrow{\text{x 50}}$ ___

(2) 10 $\xrightarrow{\text{x 10}}$ ___

(3) 8 $\xrightarrow{\text{x 10}}$ ___

(4) 3 $\xrightarrow{\text{x 20}}$ ___

(5) 5 $\xrightarrow{\text{x 20}}$ ___

(6) 4 $\xrightarrow{\text{x 25}}$ ___

(7) ___ $\xleftarrow{\text{x 2}}$ 40

(8) ___ $\xleftarrow{\text{x 20}}$ 5

(9) 20 $\xrightarrow{\text{x 5}}$ ___

(10) ___ $\xrightarrow{\text{x 50}}$ 100

(11) ___ $\xleftarrow{\text{x 10}}$ 7

(12) 25 $\xrightarrow{\text{x 3}}$ ___

(13) 25 $\xrightarrow{\text{x 4}}$ ___

(14) ___ $\xleftarrow{\text{x 5}}$ 10

(15) 3 $\xrightarrow{\text{x 10}}$ ___

(16) ___ $\xleftarrow{\text{x 25}}$ 2

(17) ___ $\xleftarrow{\text{x 10}}$ 4

(18) 2 $\xrightarrow{\text{x 20}}$ ___

(19) 100 $\xleftarrow{\text{x 25}}$ ___

(20) ___ $\xrightarrow{\text{x 10}}$ 100

(21) 100 $\xleftarrow{\text{x 5}}$ ___

(22) ___ $\xrightarrow{\text{x 20}}$ 100

(23) ___ $\xrightarrow{\text{x 25}}$ 75

(24) 70 $\xleftarrow{\text{x 10}}$ ___

(25) ___ $\xrightarrow{\text{x 4}}$ 100

(26) ___ $\xrightarrow{\text{x 5}}$ 100

(27) 80 $\xleftarrow{\text{x 4}}$ ___

(28) 100 $\xleftarrow{\text{x 2}}$ ___

(29) 50 $\xleftarrow{\text{x 10}}$ ___

(30) ___ $\xrightarrow{\text{x 10}}$ 60

Teach your student to check their answers. Your student can now convert fractions with denominators 2, 4, 5, 10, 20, 25, and 50 to percents using the arrow method (for other denominators they must use cross-multiplication).

Example: Change $3/5$ to a percent.

$$\frac{3}{5} \rightarrow \frac{3}{5} = \frac{}{100} \xrightarrow{\times 20} \frac{3}{5} = \frac{}{100} \xrightarrow{\times 20} \overset{\times 20}{\frac{3}{5}} \xrightarrow{} \frac{60}{100} = 60\%$$

Have your student convert the following decimals to percents (by first converting to a fraction):

(1) .7   (2) .25   (3) .3   (4) .72

Have your student write the percent of the following diagrams that is shaded:

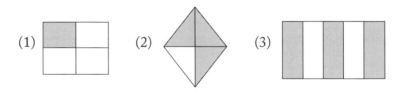

RP-8: Finding Ratios and Percents

(This section is for second-year JUMP students)

The sentence "6 is $^2/_3$ of 9" is equivalent to the mathematical expression $^2/_3 = ^6/_9$.

Example: Rewrite "8 is $^2/_3$ of 12" as an equality.

Step 1: Write the fraction given beside an equal sign:

$$\frac{2}{3} =$$

Step 2: Write the number that follows the word "of" on the bottom:

$$\frac{2}{3} = \frac{}{12}$$

Step 3: Fill in the other number:

$$\frac{2}{3} = \frac{8}{12}$$

Make sure your student knows that the number that follows the word "of" *always* goes on the bottom — 12 is the *whole* that you are taking two-thirds of.

Have your student rewrite the following statements as equalities:

(1) "3 is $^1\!/_2$ of 6"   (2) "4 is $^2\!/_3$ of 6"   (3) "9 is $^3\!/_4$ of 12"

(4) "10 is $^2\!/_3$ of 15"   (5) "15 is $^3\!/_4$ of 20"   (6) "7 is $^1\!/_3$ of 21"

(7) "12 is $^3\!/_4$ of 16"   (8) "9 is $^3\!/_5$ of 15"

Your student can also write percent statements as equalities.

Example: Write "3 is 75% of 4" as an equality.

First change 75% to a fraction ($^{75}\!/_{100}$), then use the method above:

$$\frac{75}{100} = \frac{3}{4}$$

Have your student rewrite the following as equalities:

(1) "2 is 40% of 5"   (2) "7 is 70% of 10"   (3) "3 is 60% of 5"

(4) "1 is 25% of 4"   (5) "3 is 6% of 50"   (6) "20 is 80% of 25"

Your student can now find missing numbers in ratios and percent statements.

Type 1: What number is $^3\!/_4$ of 20?

Write the fraction beside an equal sign:

$$\frac{3}{4} =$$

Fill in the number after "of" and solve by the arrow method:

$$\frac{3}{4} = \frac{\quad}{20}$$ ("of" indicates 20 goes on the bottom)

Ask your student to solve the following:

(1) What number is $^2/_3$ of 12?   (2) What number is $^3/_4$ of 8?

(3) What number is $^2/_5$ of 20?   (4) What number is $^1/_3$ of 12?

(5) What number is $^2/_3$ of 21?   (6) What number is $^4/_5$ of 25?

Type 2: 8 is $^2/_3$ of what number?

This time, the number following the "of" is missing (we don't know the whole of which 8 is two-thirds). Hence the blank goes on the bottom:

$$\frac{2}{3} = \frac{8}{\quad}$$

Ask your student to solve the following:

(1) 6 is $^2/_3$ of what number?   (2) 15 is $^3/_4$ of what number?

(3) 6 is $^3/_5$ of what number?   (4) 10 is $^2/_3$ of what number?

(5) 7 is $^1/_3$ of what number?   (6) 9 is $^3/_4$ of what number?

Type 3: 4 is how many thirds of 6?

This time we don't know the fraction:

$$\frac{}{3} = \frac{4}{6}$$

Have your student solve the following:

(1) 8 is how many fifths of 10?   (2) 4 is how many quarters of 12?

(3) 15 is how many quarters of 20? (4) 6 is how many thirds of 9?

Your student should be able to solve the three types of questions even if they are mixed together:

(1) What number is $\frac{1}{5}$ of 20?   (2) 5 is $\frac{1}{3}$ of what number?

(3) 9 is how many quarters of 12?   (4) 14 is how many thirds of 21?

(5) What number is $\frac{2}{3}$ of 15?   (6) 6 is $\frac{2}{3}$ of what number?

(7) 10 is $\frac{5}{6}$ of what number?   (8) 2 is how many thirds of 6?

Make up other questions of this sort by starting with a pair of equivalent fractions, and then leaving one number out. Make sure your student can articulate, as soon as they have read the question, what is missing — for instance, in the first question above, the *part* is missing:

$$\frac{1}{5} = \frac{}{20} \quad \longleftarrow \quad \text{part}$$

In the second question, the *whole* is missing:

$$\frac{1}{3} = \frac{5}{\quad} \longleftarrow \text{whole}$$

In the third question, the *fraction* is missing:

$$\frac{\quad}{4} = \frac{9}{12}$$

This method also works for percents.

Example: What number is 20% of 5?

Rewrite the percent as a fraction:

What number is 20% of 5?

$$\frac{20}{100}$$

Then solve by arrows:

$$\frac{20}{100} = \frac{\quad}{5} \qquad \frac{20}{100} \underset{\times 20}{\overset{\times 20}{=}} 5 \qquad \frac{20}{100} = \frac{1}{5}$$

Example: 4 is what percent of 5?

The percent is missing: $\longrightarrow \dfrac{\quad}{100} = \dfrac{4}{5}$ Then solve.

Have your student solve the following:

(1) 3 is 60% of what number?   (2) 4 is what percent of 5?

(3) 7 is what percent of 10?   (4) 1 is 25% of what number?

Make up similar problems by starting with equivalent fractions:

$$\frac{3}{4} = \frac{75}{100} \quad \text{etc.}$$

Sometimes your student will encounter slightly different wording:

"Find 20% of 5."

The word "of" *always* signals the number that goes on the bottom, for example,

$$\frac{20}{100} = \frac{}{5}$$

Example: "What percent *of* 60 is 40?"

$$\frac{}{100} = \frac{40}{60}$$

Example: "How many thirds *of* 9 is 6?"

$$\frac{}{3} = \frac{6}{9}$$

Make up problems with more difficult wording only after your student has mastered the standard wording.

CHAPTER 10

Logic and Systematic Search

IN MATHEMATICS TEXTS USED IN ELEMENTARY SCHOOLS, STUDENTS are frequently required to solve problems of the following sort: Find all shapes that can be made using five squares (assuming that each square has at least one edge in common with another square). While there are only 12 distinct (non-congruent) shapes that can be made from five squares, there are over 100 ways of drawing or placing the squares without violating the conditions of the question. As teachers are not adequately trained to show a student how to sort through this many possible configurations (and a typical textbook will offer little or no guidance in organizing such a search), an elementary student is unlikely to find all 12 of the shapes that can be made with five squares. They are even less likely to know how to verify whether their set of solutions is complete.

Many discoveries in mathematics are made by the process of elimination: a mathematician lists all of the possible answers to a question (or, more often, the most promising answers), checking to see if any are valid. A knack for solving problems by systematic search is essential in mathematics, but I have never seen a book that isolates this skill. In this unit, your student will learn how to solve problems by listing potential solutions in an organized way.

Note: You needn't teach this unit all at once — the exercises can be interspersed with other units.

LS-1: Lists

To find a number that satisfies several conditions simultaneously, you can start by making a list of numbers that satisfy one of the conditions, then check to see which numbers on the list satisfy the other conditions. Make sure your student is aware of this rule: you might point out, for instance, that the lists they make in parts g to l of question 2 can be used to solve parts m to u.

Your student should know that the multiples of any number include 0 (e.g., the multiples of 2 are 0, 2, 4, 6, etc.) and that the even numbers also include 0.

1. Write the numbers from 0 to 9 in order.

2. Write all the numbers from 0 to 9 that are
   a) greater than 7
   b) less than 2
   c) greater than 5
   d) less than 8
   e) greater than 5 and less than 8
   f) less than 5 and greater than 0
   g) odd numbers
   h) even numbers
   i) multiples of 2
   j) multiples of 3
   k) multiples of 4
   l) multiples of 5

m) odd numbers greater than 5
n) even numbers greater than 7
o) odd numbers less than 5
p) even numbers less than 4
q) even numbers that are multiples of 4
r) odd numbers that are multiples of 3

BONUS

s) even numbers that are greater than 2 and less than 8
t) odd numbers that are greater than 1 and less than 7
u) odd numbers that are multiples of 3 and greater than 5

3. Write the numbers from 0 to 9 in order, then:
   a) Circle the number that is greater than 8
   b) Underline the number that is less than 1
   c) Cross out the number that is less than 8 and greater than 6
   d) Put a check mark over the odd number that is greater than 3 and less than 7

4. Use the clues to find the answers: "I am a *one-digit* number. I am ..."
   a) greater than 8
   b) less than 1
   c) greater than 6 and less than 8
   d) an odd number greater than 7
   e) an odd number less than 3
   f) an even number greater than 6
   g) an even number less than 1
   h) an odd number greater than 3, and less than 6
   i) an even number greater than 2, and less than 6

BONUS

    k) the second odd number

    l) a multiple of 3 greater than 6

    m) a multiple of 5 greater than 1

5. Use the clues to find the answers: "I am a *two-digit* number . . ."
   a) My tens digit is 9 and my units digit is 1.
   b) My units digit is 5 and my tens digit is 7.
   c) My units digit is 0 and my tens digit is 4.
   d) My units digit is 5. Both of my digits are the same.
   e) My tens digit is 7. My units digit is 2 less than my tens digit.
   f) My units digit is 2. My tens digit is 3 more than my units digit.
   g) My tens digit is 6. My units digit is 5 less than my tens digit.
   h) My tens digit is 7. The sum of my digits is 9.

6. All of these questions have *more than one* answer. List all of the solutions: "I am a *two-digit* number . . ."
   a) The sum of my digits is 2.
   b) The sum of my digits is 3.
   c) The sum of my digits is 4.
   d) The sum of my digits is 5.
   e) The sum of my digits is 6.
   f) Both of my digits are the same.
   g) My units digit is 5. I am less than 40.
   h) My tens digit is twice my units digit.
   i) My tens digit is 3 times my units digit.

7. All of these questions have only *one* answer. Read the first sentence and list all possible answers. Then read the second sentence and circle the correct answer: "I am a *two-digit* number . . ."
   a) The sum of my digits is 2. Both of my digits are the same.
   b) The sum of my digits is 3. My units digit is twice my tens digit.
   c) The sum of my digits is 3. My tens digit is greater than 2.
   d) The sum of my digits is 4. Both of my digits are the same.
   e) The sum of my digits is 5. My tens digit is one more than my units digit.
   f) The sum of my digits is 5. My tens digit is 3 less than my units digit.
   g) Both of my digits are the same. I am greater than 50 and less than 60.
   h) Both of my digits are the same. I am greater than 90.
   i) Both of my digits are the same. If you multiply my digits you get 9.
   j) Both of my digits are the same. The sum of my digits is 12.

8. All of these questions have *more than one* answer. In each question there is a sentence that tells you what one of the digits of the answer must be. Underline this sentence. Then write all of the answers. "I am a *two-digit* number . . ."
   a) My units digit is 7. My tens digit is even.
   b) My units digit is odd. My tens digit is 5.
   c) I am between 40 and 50. My units digit is odd.
   d) My units digit is a multiple of 3. I am between 70 and 80.
   e) I am between 20 and 30. My units digit is a multiple of 3.
   f) I am greater than 90. My units digit is a multiple of 4.
   g) My tens digit is even. My units digit is greater than 6 and less than 8.
   h) My ones digit is odd. My tens digit is greater than 4 and less than 6.

9. What is the hundreds digit of a *three-digit* number:
   a) between 400 and 500?
   b) between 200 and 300?
   c) greater than 900?
   d) less than 200?

10. All of these questions have *more than one* answer. List all of the answers. "I am a *three-digit* number . . ."
   a) I am greater than 900. My tens digit is 2 times my units digit.
   b) I am between 400 and 500. My units digit is 5 more than my tens digit.
   c) I am between 200 and 300. My tens digit is 3 more than my units digit.
   d) I am less than 200. My tens digit is 4 less than my units digit.

11. All of these questions have *one* answer. "I am a *three-digit* number . . ."
   a) I am between 500 and 600. All of my digits are the same.
   b) I am between 200 and 300. My units digit is 3 times my hundreds digit. The sum of my digits is 10.
   c) My hundreds digit, 9, is 3 times my units digit. The sum of my digits is 14.
   d) My units digit, 8, is 2 times my tens digit and 4 times my hundreds digit.
   e) I am between 800 and 900. My hundreds digit is 2 times my ones digit. The sum of my digits is 15.
   f) I am between 800 and 900. My hundreds digit is 4 times my tens digit. The sum of my digits is 14.
   g) I am between 300 and 400. My tens digit and my units digit are the same. The sum of my digits is 9.

h) I am between 400 and 500. The digit in each place is one greater than the digit on its left.
i) All of my digits are the same. The sum of my digits is 15.

Advanced

The following questions are more advanced. You might wait until your student is in the second year of JUMP before you cover this material.

In questions 12 and 13, you should tell your student to draw as many lines as there are digits in the number; they can then fill in the blanks using the clues. (Teach your students to put a comma after every three blanks; it will help them see the places.) Your student should know that the units digit of a number is also called "the first digit," the tens digit is "the second digit," and so on. The first three digits are "the units period," and the next three digits are "the thousands period."

12. The following questions have *one* answer. "I am a *four-digit* number . . ."
    a) I am less than 2,000. The digits in my units period are all the same. The sum of my digits is 7.
    b) All of my digits are the same. The sum of my digits is 20.
    d) I am less than 4,000. All of my digits are multiples of 3. My second and fourth digit are the same. My units digit and my hundreds digit are 6 more than the others.
    e) My thousands digit is greater than 6 and is 2 times my hundreds digit. My other digits are odd numbers greater than 7.

Before you assign question 13, make sure your student knows the names of the places up to the hundred millions. Point out to your student that when a number has five digits and is less than, say, 40,000, there are several possibilities for the leading digit (i.e., it might be 3, 2 or 1).

BONUS

13. Answer the following questions:

   a) I am a five-digit number less than 30,000. The digit in each place is one greater than the digit on its left. The sum of my digits is 15.

   b) I am a number between 400,000 and 500,000. The digits in my thousands period are all the same. The digits in my units period are all the same. The sum of my digits is 18.

   c) I am a six-digit number. The digits in my thousands period are all 2s. The digits in my units period are all the same. The sum of my digits is 15.

   d) I am a seven-digit number. My millions digit 4, is 2 times my units digit. My thousands digit is three times my units digit. The sum of my digits is 12.

   e) I am an eight-digit number between 34 million and 35 million. The digits in my thousands period are all 0s. The digits in my units period are all the same. The sum of my digits is 13.

   f) I am a nine-digit, odd number. The sum of my digits is 2.

LS-2: Systematic Search

A mathematician will sometimes gain insight into a challenging problem by inventing a "toy" model of the problem, a version of the problem that has all of the essential features of the original, but fewer elements or parameters. In teaching mathematics, it helps to employ a similar strategy. If my student is struggling with a problem, I will look for a model or sequence of models in which the concepts underlying the problem are isolated or introduced in steps. In this section I present some examples of how I would make toy models to teach more difficult problems.

I recently came across the following exercise in a Grade 8 book: "You have six boxes numbered 1 to 6. Show all the ways you can build two towers three blocks high so that a block with a lower number never appears above a block with a higher number." If you think your student would have trouble finding (or verifying that they have found) all the solutions to this problem, you could start with the following sequence of questions.

Ask your student to imagine that they have three boxes numbered 1, 2, and 3. Have them draw a picture showing all the ways they could make a stack of two boxes in which a box with a lower number never appears above a box with a higher number. Their answer should have three stacks:

2		3		3
1		1		2

If your student needs help, ask them whether the box with label 3 could ever appear on the bottom of a stack. Point out that they won't miss any solutions if they proceed in a systematic way. They could put box 1 on the bottom, placing the other boxes on top, one at a time, in order, from least to greatest. Then they could put box 2 on the bottom (and so on, if there are more boxes). Ask your student to use this method to show all the ways they could make a stack that is two boxes high using four boxes (with the rule that a lower number can never appear above a higher number). Then have them list all the ways they can make:

a) a stack two boxes high using five boxes
b) a stack three boxes high using four boxes
c) a stack three boxes high using six boxes

In each of the examples above, I used the numbers on the boxes to help organize my search for solutions. This simple trick (using the order of the natural numbers to list all possibilities) can be employed to solve a wide variety of problems. A student asked to find all pairs of whole numbers that add to 18 might start their list with the number 1 (1 +17 = 18), then the number 2 (2 + 16 = 18), and so on. As long as the student doesn't skip any numbers in counting, they can be certain they have found all pairs. Similarly, a student asked to find the dimensions of all rectangles with perimeter 18 units (sides are assumed to have lengths that are whole numbers) could begin by calculating the length of a rectangle with width 1 unit, then the length of a rectangle with width 2 units, and so on.

On provincial math tests in Ontario, a great many elementary students fail to find complete solutions to questions of the sort I have mentioned above. I find it surprising that textbooks don't teach students how to order their search for solutions by counting: once this method is learned it becomes automatic.

Here are several types of questions that can be solved using the ordering method I have described. (All sides of geometric figures have lengths that are whole numbers.)

1. Find the dimensions of all rectangles with perimeter 24 units.

2. Find the dimensions of all rectangles with area 12 units.

3. List the factors of 12. (Ask your student why this question and the previous question have the same set of solutions.)

4. Find the dimensions of all triangles with perimeter 13. (Remember, three numbers can only be the lengths of sides of a proper triangle if the sum of any pair of the numbers is greater than the third number. Hence, 1, 1 and 11 cannot be the lengths of the sides of a triangle, as 1 + 1 is less than 11.)

The fourth question is more difficult than the other three. It may be broken into a series of simpler questions. For instance, you might ask: Suppose one of the sides of the triangle has length 3 units. Find all possible lengths for the other two sides.

In elementary schools, students are expected to solve problems of the following type: Find all the ways you can make $1.14 using pennies, dimes, and dollars. If you think your student would have trouble verifying that they have found all solutions to this problem, start with a problem that involves only two types of coins, such as: How many ways can you make 25 cents using pennies and dimes? Tell your student to list their answers in a chart. Your student may discover on their own that the best way to list answers is to start with none of the largest coin (in this case dimes), then one of the largest coin, and so on. Point out that when the number of dimes is fixed, the number of pennies is also determined.

Dimes	Pennies
0	25
1	15
2	5

When your student is able to solve any problem involving two coins, they can move on the problem of making $1.14 with pennies, dimes, and dollars. As with problems involving only two coins, it helps to assume that you have none of the larger coin first (so that the problem is reduced to the problem of making $1.14 using pennies and dimes), then one of the larger coin (now the problem is reduced to the problem of making 14 cents using pennies and dimes). As with the previous example, your student can keep track of their answers in a chart:

Dollars	**Dimes**	**Pennies**
0	0	114
0	1	104
0	2	94
0	3	84
0	4	74
0	5	64
0	6	54
0	7	44
0	8	34
0	9	24
0	10	14
0	11	4
1	0	14
1	1	4

Problems involving systematic search turn up in every branch of mathematics, including geometry. Here are some simple problems that teach the concepts of perimeter and congruence (two figures are congruent if they have exactly the same shape and size).

1. Write the perimeter of each figure in the sequence (assume each edge is 1 unit).

   How does the perimeter change each time a square is added?

   If the sequence were continued, what would the perimeter of the seventh figure be?

2. Write the perimeter of each figure in the sequence below:

   How does the perimeter change each time a hexagon is added?

   If the sequence were continued, what would the perimeter of the sixth figure be?

3. a) Add a square so that the number of exterior edges increases by 2:

   b) Add a square so that the number of exterior edges stays the same:

4. Is it possible to add a square to the figure in question 5a so that the number of exterior edges increases by 3 (assuming whole edges must fit together exactly)?

5. Find the perimeter of each figure. Then add one square to the figure so that the perimeter of the new figure is 10 units. (In questions 5 to 8 below, assume all edges are 1 unit.)

a)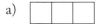

b)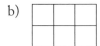

c)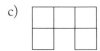

6. Find the perimeter of each figure. Then add one more triangle to the figure so that the perimeter of the new figure is 6 units.

a)

b)

7. Add squares to this figure so that the perimeter is 18

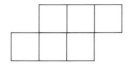

8. Add two squares to the figure so that . . .

. . . its perimeter
stays the same

. . . its perimeter
increases by 2 units

9. Show how many different (non-congruent) shapes you can make by adding *one* square to the figure. (The square you add must share an edge with a square in the original figure.)

a)   b)   c)   d)

10. Show how many different (non-congruent) shapes you can make by adding *two* squares.

a)   b)   c)   d)

11. How many different shapes can you make using
   a) three squares?
   b) four squares?

Once your student has successfully completed the exercises above, they should be ready to tackle the problem I mentioned at the beginning of this chapter, namely: Find all shapes you can make using five squares. (Your student should look for solutions to this problem by adding a single square, in various positions, to the figures they made in question 11b.)

LS-3: Puzzles

As your student becomes more adept at systematic search, you can introduce them to more challenging mathematical puzzles. Here are several examples of puzzles that require a good deal of search by trial and error.

1. Place the numbers 1, 2, 3, 4, 5, and 6 in the boxes and circles so that the number in each circle is equal to the sum of the two numbers in the boxes nearest to the circle.

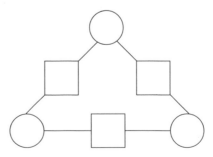

In this question, you can teach your student how to eliminate possibilities before they start: for instance, you might ask, "Are there any numbers that can't be placed in the circles?" Your student should see that neither 1 nor 2 can be placed in the circles, as no pair of numbers will add to 1 or 2. This means 1 and 2 must be placed in a pair of boxes, and that 3, therefore, must be placed in the adjacent circle.

If you think your student is ready for more challenging work, you could give them the following questions:

2. Place the numbers 1, 2, 3, 4, 5, and 6 so that the three numbers along each edge add to:

   a) 10
   b) 11
   c) 12

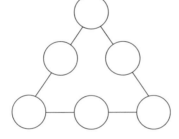

3. Place the numbers 1, 2, 3, 4, 5, 6, and 7 so that the three numbers along each line, including the diagonals, add to the same number.

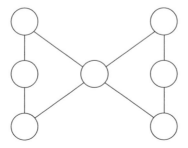

LS-4: Additional Exercises

1. With coins or a picture, show all the ways you can make the following amounts using nickels and dimes:
   a) 10 cents
   b) 15 cents
   c) 20 cents
   d) 25 cents

2. With coins or a picture, show four ways you can make the following amounts using nickels, dimes, and quarters:
   a) 25 cents
   b) 30 cents
   c) 60 cents

3. Crayons come in boxes of 4 or 5. For each of the following numbers, can you buy a combination of boxes that will give you the number exactly? (For some of these questions, you needn't buy boxes of both types.)
   a) 8 crayons
   b) 10 crayons
   c) 11 crayons
   d) 14 crayons
   e) 17 crayons
   f) 18 crayons
   g) 19 crayons
   h) 21 crayons
   i) 25 crayons

4. In each of the following questions, your student should fill in the blanks with the digits from 0 to 9 (in each question, they can only use each digit once). Make:

a) The greatest number __ __

b) The least number __ __

c) The least odd number __ __

d) The greatest number with 9 in the tens place __ __ __

e) The greatest even number with 4 in the thousands place __ __ __ __

f) The greatest odd number with 7 in the thousands place __ __ __ __

g) The least even number greater than 30,000 __ __ __ __ __

5. Pick two numbers, one from each of the boxes so that:
   a) the product of the two numbers is smallest
   b) the product is the greatest
   c) the product is closest to 20
   d) the difference between the two numbers is smallest

```
┌─────────┐   ┌─────────┐
│  7      │   │  3      │
│      5  │   │      2  │
│  1      │   │  9      │
└─────────┘   └─────────┘
```

CHAPTER 11

Finite State Automata

I N THIS UNIT, YOUR STUDENT WILL LEARN HOW TO MAKE A FINITE state automaton, a simple model of a computer, which can be played like a board game. Though the model has no wires or circuits (your student will have to supply the "electricity"), it can perform several of the same functions as a real computer. By feeding code words into the automaton, your student will learn how a computer performs basic tasks, such as identifying patterns in numbers and codes.

FS-1: Codes

Computers follow instructions that are encoded in strings of letters or numbers called "words." The words that tell a computer what to do are generally written using only two symbols. This is because the presence of an electrical current in a wire or circuit can represent the occurrence of one of the symbols, and the absence of current, the other. The symbols most commonly used in computer science are "0" and "1."

To give your student an idea of how instructions may be encoded in strings of zeroes and ones, you should write down the following code:

A = 0   B = 1   C = 00

D = 01   E = 11   F = 000

G = 001   H = 011   I = 111

Ask your student to continue the pattern in the code. They should notice that each new "word" in the code is generated either by replacing the rightmost zero of the previous word with a one, or, if the previous word consists entirely of ones, by creating a string of zeroes one longer than the string of ones. Hence, the pattern continues as follows:

J = 0000   K = 0001   L = 0011

M = 0111   etc.

Show your student how to translate a code word into English by writing the corresponding letter of the alphabet under each block of code. For instance,

000 0 00 11 = 000 0 00 11
            F A C E

Ask your student to decode the following words:

(1) 1 0 01   (2) 000 11 11 01   (3) 1 11 01

(4) 1 11 0 01   (5) 00 0 1   (6) 1 0 001

(If your student enjoys working with codes, have them translate a word that contains letters that occur near the end of the alphabet. This will require extending the code further than what is provided above.)

A *binary* code is one that uses only two symbols. The code given above is not, strictly speaking, binary, since it allows for a space between blocks of symbols. (From the point of view of a computer, a space is a third symbol.) You might ask your student to think about how they would design a code that does not require a space. Here is an example of such a code:

A = 010   B = 0110   C = 01110

D = 011110   etc.

It is easy to spot the letters of the alphabet in words written in binary code, as each letter is represented by a block of ones, flanked by a pair of zeroes. For instance, in "0110010011110" the letters b, a, and d stand out.

Ask your student to simplify the code I have just given. (One way to simplify the code is to drop the final zero in each word: the code still works if A is written 01, B is written 011, etc.)

FS-2: Finite State Automata

In the code given above, the word "000000" is meaningless, as it does not correspond to any letter or series of letters in the English alphabet. A computer can only follow instructions that are correctly written in the specific code the computer uses. In order to process and execute instructions, a computer must be able to recognize various kinds of patterns in strings of symbols.

In this section, your student will learn how to design an automaton that can "read" and recognize patterns in binary words. Such automata are important components of most computers.

A finite state automaton consists of a set of circles labelled with numbers, and a set of arrows labelled with the letters "a" and "b." (Automata with more than two types of labels on their arrows are equivalent in computing power to those with only two types of label, so we will only consider automata of the latter sort.) A circle is called a "state," while a pair of concentric circles is called an "accept state." The automaton below has three states. The state labelled with a "0" is an accept state.

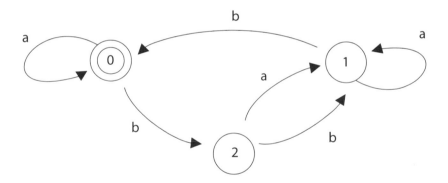

In an automaton, exactly two arrows must originate from each state. One of the two arrows must be labelled with an "a" and the other with a "b." An arrow from a state must either point to another state or to the state where it originated. In the diagram above, the "b" arrow originating at state 0 points to state 2, while the "a" arrow loops back and points to state 0 itself.

Ask your student to copy the finite state automaton given above onto a piece of paper. Place a penny or marker on the zero state of their picture. Then give your student a word written in the letters "a" and "b."

(The states of an automaton are normally labelled with numbers, but I have chosen to write words using the letters "a" and "b," rather than zeroes and ones: students find this less confusing.) Tell your student to read the word you gave them from left to right, one letter at a time. Each time they read a letter, they should move the penny along the arrow labelled by the letter they have just read. For instance, if you were to give your student the word "baa," they would move the penny from state 0 to 2, from state 2 to 1, and then from state 1 to state 1 (i.e., on the final move, the penny remains in the same state, because the arrow labelled "a" loops back to that state).

A finite state automaton can either accept or reject a word. Normally, finite state automata are designed to accept only those words that are meaningful or "well formed" in whatever code the computer uses. In our penny model of a finite state automaton, words are accepted or rejected as follows: if, when the final letter of the word is read, the penny lands in an accept state of the automaton, the word is accepted. Otherwise, it is rejected. In the example given above, the word "baa" is rejected, as state 1 is not an accept state.

Have your student try other words on the automaton until they get used to moving the penny around as they read a word. You should give them a list and have them check which words the computer accepts. Then show them the following automaton and ask them to try to figure out what kind of words it accepts:

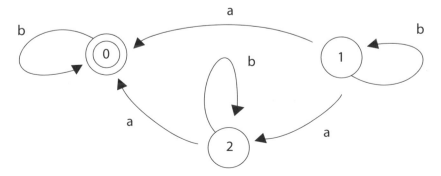

You might give them some hints: for instance, you might point out that an occurrence of "b" in a word always leaves the penny in the same state, since all of the "b" arrows are loops. You might give your student a word with three a's, then one with six a's. They should see that the automata accepts any word in which the number of a's is a multiple of 3 (the number of b's doesn't matter). Ask your student to draw an automaton that will accept any word in which the number of a's is a multiple of 5. Then ask them to figure out what kinds of words each of the following automata will accept.

1.

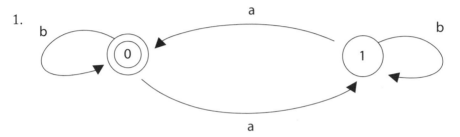

This automaton accepts words that have an even number of a's.

2.

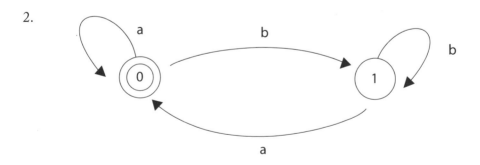

This automaton accepts words that end in one or more a's.

3.

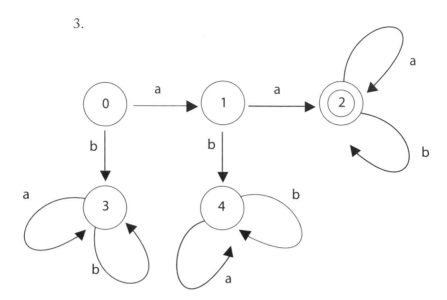

This automaton accepts words that start with exactly two a's.

The following questions are more advanced:

4.

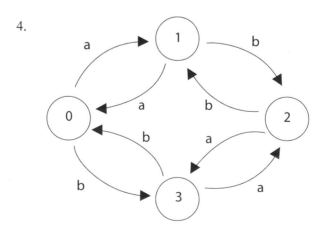

This automaton accepts words that have an even number of a's and also an even number of b's.

Automata may also have more than one accept state, as in the following:

5.

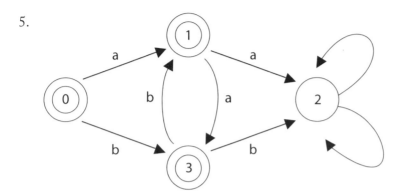

This automaton accepts words that don't have two a's or two b's in a row.

You might ask your student to design their own automaton and, if possible, determine what kinds of words it accepts. The question of what kinds of words automata can recognize is a very deep and important question in computer science.

FS-3: Codes for Automata

A finite state automaton may be represented by a set of brackets containing letters and symbols. The brackets and symbols are a code that tells you how to construct a particular automaton. In each bracket, there are three positions. The first position contains a state number, the second a letter (either "a" or "b"), and the third, another state number. For instance, the bracket (1,a,2) means that in the automata, there is an arrow labelled "a" from state 1 to state 2 (or, interpreted as an instruction, the bracket means that if the penny is in state 1 and you read an "a," you should move the penny to state 2). A description of an automaton should also specify which of the states of the automata are "accept" states.

The following "code" gives the program for the automaton on page 197:

(0,a,0) (0,b,2) (1,a,1) (1,b,0) (2,a,1) (2,b,1)

where 0 is the accept state.

Write a code for one of the automata above and ask your student to draw a picture of the automaton from the code. Then have your student write the code for an automaton from its diagram.

Note: Several months ago, after a lesson on finite state automata, my daughter Chloe decided she would make her own model of a computer. She found a shallow box with a Cellophane lid and put a drawing of an automaton inside. Then, rather than using a penny as a marker, she placed a round fridge magnet on the zero state of her automaton and used a second magnet on the back of the box to pull the other magnet around like a cursor. She drew a keyboard for her computer, along with several Web pages and games (mazes and so on). When Chloe demonstrated her model to a Grade 3 class in the JUMP program, all of the kids wanted to make their own computers. I gave them cardboard folders instead of boxes, and they used paper clips to hold their drawings in place while they moved the magnets around. Many of the children mentioned this lesson in their thank-you letters to JUMP: in their minds, they had made real computers.

Afterword

NOT LONG AGO I BROKE UP A FIGHT AT A SCHOOL WHERE I WAS tutoring by telling the boy who started the fight to apologize or I wouldn't give him his bonus question. Perhaps the most surprising thing about this incident was not that the boy was willing to apologize to receive extra work, but that the work itself was in mathematics.

In my experience, children want two things in order to be happy at school: to exercise their minds and to show off. Mathematics may well be the subject in which children can most easily satisfy both of these desires.

Before children can read, they must acquire an extraordinary number of visual, auditory, and cognitive skills. But children can master a great deal of mathematics simply by counting on their fingers (something we have evolved to excel at).

As I am not a psychologist, I can't say why the method of teaching used in JUMP has such a remarkable effect on children who have trouble learning. Perhaps the thrill of success and the intense mental effort required to remember complex rules and carry out long chains of computation and inference develops parts of their minds they normally are incapable of using. (Lately I have even observed growth in motor and perceptual abilities in children who have completed the fractions unit.) I suspect that a remedial reading program would be more successful if preceded by or coupled with a JUMP-style math program. I also suspect that JUMP could significantly help children who have trouble with socialization: I have witnessed children diagnosed as autistic or selective mutes regularly call out answers in class after only a month or two of lessons.

If math is the subject in which students can succeed most easily (and thereby can develop the cognitive abilities and the confidence they need to succeed in other subjects), then our failure to teach math to the majority of students is all the more deplorable.

I would be extremely disappointed, however, if this book caused even one parent to pester their child's teacher with unreasonable demands. Teachers are largely responsible for the success of JUMP: they have welcomed the program into their classes because they are dedicated to helping their students. Rather than harassing a teacher (who is likely overworked, underpaid, and on the verge of quitting), a parent who wishes to improve our schools should consider volunteering in a class or pressuring governments to provide training for teachers as well as tutors for students who need extra help. (This is not as costly as it sounds: one or two full-time tutors, assisting trained teachers, could take care of an entire school.)

Teachers, on the other hand, must open their minds to the fact that, with proper teaching, all children can learn math. I recently worked with a teacher who told me I shouldn't waste my time with his weakest students as they had mild intellectual delays. After I had tutored those children for several months, the teacher changed his mind: he is now one of the most enthusiastic supporters of the program.

Historically, societies have always been divided by myths of difference: between peasants and nobility, slaves and slave owners, or minorities and majorities. Today, the most pervasive and enduring of those myths — the myth of ability — is being challenged. People who traditionally would not work together have found common cause in JUMP. Our volunteers include vice-presidents of banks and social activists. Regardless of their political beliefs, people who have seen children flourish in JUMP find it easy to agree that children are more alike intellectually then they seem.

I am not advocating a society without challenges, where exceptional achievement goes unnoticed. But the tests a society offers its members, particularly when they are young, should be designed to elevate the human spirit, not crush it.

Recently I gave a lesson in mathematics to class of students at the York Detention Centre in Toronto. I was rather nervous before the lesson started, not only because the members of the class were all awaiting trial, but also because I had no idea how teenagers would respond to a method of teaching I had only tried with children. It didn't help when I heard a girl mutter, "I'm not doing this," or when a guard stopped me from lending a boy my pencil because it hadn't been counted and might be smuggled out of the class as a weapon.

After an hour, the students had all completed ten pages of work. The girl I had heard complaining called me over to her table. I told her she shouldn't expect me to mark all ten pages: I could tell, from the questions I had checked during the lesson, that she had gotten everything right. But she insisted that I put a check mark beside every one of her answers. When I had finished she said, "I've never had that in my life. I've only had this . . ." and she wrote a large X across her page.

As the guards gathered and counted the pencils, and the students were escorted to their cells, it seemed to me that we were all involved in an absurd mistake: the teenagers had spent the hour calling for the instructors to mark their answers and demanding more challenging work. They had responded exactly as I have seen children respond to the promise that they would succeed.

When I was a child, I believed that one day I would travel in time. But time escorted me, quickly and irreversibly, into a life I could scarcely have imagined. I had hoped I would grow up to be a great mathematician, or the author of a book better than this. But I have come to believe in my abilities rather late.

We all have abilities that were neglected in the past and that we now are unlikely to develop. But we might still accomplish more as a society than all the towering geniuses of the past. For if we were merely to educate our children, we would be the last generation whose promise was lost.

Acknowledgements

JUMP GREW OUT OF MY EXPERIENCE TEACHING IN A VOLUNTEER program founded by Ken and Inez Johnson. Ken is a school teacher, and Inez, a principal. Inez Johnson and Silvana Carletti were the first principals to invite JUMP into their schools as an after-school program.

Kathy Love, a special-education teacher, has devoted countless hours to organizing and overseeing the program at her school. She and David Fontaine, a teacher, first suggested we try JUMP in the classroom. Jean Kosloff taught with me during the test of the in-class program described in Chapter 4. Theresa Koch, a teacher, was also a major advocate for the program in its early years.

In the third year of JUMP, Maggie Licata, an engineer, donated four months of full-time work in order to establish JUMP as an organization. She became the first executive director of JUMP.

Inez Johnson, Silvana Carletti, Leslie Moody, and Patsy Cook were the first principals to invite JUMP to try an in-class pilot program in their schools.

Katie Baldwin, Paul Green, and Natalie Krnic started the first JUMP program in a correctional facility.

The JUMP board of directors have guided JUMP's growth over the past three years. They are: Pia Marquard (chair), Mark Damelin (treasurer), Julie Dzerowicz (sectretary), Daniel Brooks, Su Hutchinson, Susan Morais, and Arlett Tygesen.

The following individuals have done a great deal of volunteer administrative and fundraising work for JUMP: David Coutanche, Leesa Blake, David Baille, Richard Michael, Martha Wilder, Fanny Lo, Ravi Negi, Joe Sinyor, Donata Frank, John Coates, Richard Wiltshire, Eric Scott, Dave Walders, the rest of the University of Toronto JUMP Chapter, Joy Abramson, Lisa Diniz, Claire Chow, Brian Marler, Nicole Brebner, Andrew Clapperton, Andy Douglas, David Young, and Jonathan Kassian. Deth (Thanou) Thirakul and Richard Michael set up the JUMP website, and Yen Chu donated her design for the JUMP logo and letterhead. Pamela Sinha helped coin the name JUMP.

The following individuals made large donations in the early years of JUMP: Janice Stein, Leslie Jones, Alan Taylor, John Coates, Bill Cain, Valerie McDonald, and Bruce Stratton.

Bradd Hart, deputy director of the Fields Institute for Research in the Mathematical Sciences, arranged for the Fields to donate office space and technical support to JUMP. All of our tutors are trained at the Fields.

The JUMP staff have done a superb job running the program and managing its growth. Full-time employees are: Lynne Patterson (executive director), Katie Baldwin (program and special projects coordinator), and Laura Miggiani (volunteer coordinator). As well, the JUMP program depends on a team of part-time, in-class trainers: Jessica Dreisziger, Jennifer Pierce, Judith De Boer, Tara Vanderwel, and Kerri MacIntosh.

Kevin Connolly and Don Bastian (both excellent editors) made many stylistic improvements to the text. Sherrie Johnson, my agent, made sure the original vision for the book was realized (even offering to publish the book herself when we couldn't find a publisher). Michael Ondaatje took the book to House of Anansi, where it was finally accepted for publication.

My daughter, Chloe Mighton, has tested most of the JUMP units and suggested improvements. She has been an inspiration for all of my work with children. Raegan Mighton encouraged me to start volunteer tutoring in the first place.

Finally, this book is dedicated to the hundreds of volunteers and students of JUMP: all of JUMP's successes are founded on your work.

ABOUT JUMP

Children are selected for JUMP (based on financial and academic need) by teachers and principals in the schools where the program operates. We regret that we do not have the resources to provide tutors or give advice on finding tutors for children outside these schools.

With very little effort, a group of motivated volunteers and teachers can transform a school or neighbourhood. If you would like to start a tutoring program modelled on JUMP, please see our website, www.jumptutoring.org .

JUMP is an extremely small charity. Our staff barely have time to meet the many commitments we have already made. We ask, therefore, that you contact JUMP directly only to volunteer or make a donation. If you plan to start your own tutoring program, please consult our website before contacting us. We are a registered charity and will issue tax receipts for donations over $10 in Canada. Donations may be made online at our website or can be sent to JUMP at 222 College Street, 2nd Floor, Toronto, ON M5T 3J1.

Chris Chapman

JOHN MIGHTON was awarded an NSERC fellowship for research in mathematics at the Fields Institute, and has taught at McMaster and the University of Toronto. He is also a Governor-General's-Award-winning playwright and appeared in the Academy-Award-winning film *Good Will Hunting*.